On Tarrying

THE
SEAGULL
LIBRARY OF
GERMAN
LITERATURE

JOSEPH VOGL

On Tarrying

TRANSLATED BY HELMUT MÜLLER-SIEVERS

LONDON NEW YORK CALCUTTA

This publication was supported by a grant
from the Goethe-Institut India

Seagull Books, 2019

Originally published as *Über das zaudern* by Joseph Vogl
© Diaphanes, Zurich-Berlin, 2007

First published in English by Seagull Books, 2011
English translation © Helmut Müller-Sievers, 2011

ISBN 978 0 8574 2 724 3

British Library Cataloguing-in-Publication Data
A catalogue record for this book is available from the British Library

Typeset by Seagull Books, Calcutta, India
Printed and bound by WordsWorth India, New Delhi, India

C O N T E N T S

TRANSLATOR'S INTRODUCTION

Sometimes a translation is better than the original. This is certainly not the case with the bulk of the present book: Joseph Vogl is renowned for the unrivalled and untranslatable suppleness and inventiveness of his German—a virtue that characterizes not only his books and essays but also his spoken and improvised discourse, as can be readily appreciated in the many television conversations with Alexander Kluge available on the web. But it just might be the case with the titular concept, tarrying. True, the German *zaudern* can boast the indexical zigzagging of its initial letter, which, significantly, it shares with other verbs in its semantic field, such as *zagen*, *zieren* and *zögern*. *Zaudern*, however, is limited to an intransitive use: you cannot *zaudern* something, whereas you certainly can tarry it. This limitation is particularly galling since the chief purpose of Vogl's essay is to show that *zaudern* has a transitive side, and that it is the progressive emergence of this transitivity that allows us to speak of a 'system', or 'programme', of tarrying. In a sense, then, Vogl anglicizes *zaudern*; he tells a story that leads from *zaudern* as passive inhibition to tarrying as transitive, if erratic, strategy. Translated or not, this essay always had English as its target language.

At the same time, however, Vogl degermanicizes 'tarrying', or at least forces us to reconsider the propositional use made of the word in philosophical literature. Doubtlessly its most prominent instance is the translation of one of those ultra-muscular sentences with which Hegel set out to shock philosophy:

> But the life of the Spirit is not the life that shrinks from death and keeps itself untouched by devastation, but rather life that endures it and maintains itself in it. It wins its truth only when, in utter dismemberment, it finds itself. [...] Spirit is this power only by looking the negative in the face, and tarrying with it. This tarrying with the negative is the magical power that converts it into being.[1]

Staring down death, tarrying with the negative—this is the Hegel that became so important to Alexandre Kojève, and, in his wake, to the French Hegelians and anti-Hegelians, including, of course, Slavoj Žižek, who devoted a book to *Tarrying with the Negative* (1993). It might not be entirely irrelevant in this context to know that Vogl is the German translator of Gilles Deleuze's *Difference and Repetition* (1968, trans. 1994), the book in which dialectic's guiding concepts are most thoroughly dismantled.

In addition to configuring the life of the Spirit as the passion of the Trinity, Hegel seeks to evoke the pathos of tragedy in those sentences about tarrying with death. Like for his roommates Hölderlin and Schelling, understanding and overcoming the problem of tragedy—in his case, sublating it into philosophy and hence into the prose of the modern world—

was an important motivation for Hegel's thought. Only if it can sound the depth of tragic abandonment, only if it can recover the nothingness of fate does philosophy have a claim to explicate reality. The passage through the confrontation with tragic destruction is, for Hegel, equivalent to the function of absolute negation in logic and therefore shows the fundamental power of dialectics as thought not only about but of the world. In the reconstruction of the *Phenomenology*, this passage through nothingness is most powerfully embodied in the drama of recognition between master and slave: if the slave tarries with the master's power to annihilate, he will not only be able to survive but also surpass the master through the knowledge of his own finitude.

Dramatic though they sound, some of Kojève's listeners, Georges Bataille first and foremost, found these passages suspicious, even laughable. Isn't there a difference between the threat of annihilation and its execution? Doesn't Hegel, for all his immersion in tragedy, single out those plays that anticipate Christian redemption (like *Oedipus Rex* and the *Oresteia*), or at least instances of meaningful sacrifice (like *Antigone*), while leaving out all those senseless deaths the majority of tragedies seem to celebrate? Is there, properly speaking, a possibility to tarry with death—does this not diminish death into a mere threat?

The German word translated by 'tarrying' in these contexts is *verweilen*. Hegel, ever sensitive to multiple layers of meaning (see *aufheben*), sees three principle factors at work in the verb. First, the sense of 'to linger': *die Weile* is that moment in time that is not subject to the 'onrush of representations' (Hölderlin); to abide in the *Weile* is to interrupt life as an expression of desire, a conundrum to which not only the *Phenomenlogy* but also its dramatic companion piece, Goethe's *Faust*, are devoted. Then there is the sense of 'to sustain': the slave, or the tragic hero, simply has to sustain and bear the threat of absolute annihilation that emanates from fate, or from the master. Synonyms are *aushalten* or *ertragen,* and it is this stratum of meaning that elicits the laughter and disdain of Bataille, Blanchot and Cie. Last, though, there is the curious form of causation that is implied in *verweilen*: the punctual *weil* (because) of efficient causality is turned into a temporal activity that confuses and multiplies reasons as it is paired with the prefix *ver-* that was so instrumental for Heidegger (*verwinden*).

It is this last sense that Vogl attempts to conserve in his replacement of *verweilen* with *zaudern*. He, too, reflects on tragedy as the context in which such confusion and multiplication of reasons has to take hold. In the chapter 'The Raised Hand', he focuses on the moment in Aeschylus' *Oresteia* when Orestes raises his hand to plunge the dagger into his mother's breast but then interrupts himself with the question, 'What should I do?' The raised and tarrying hand gathers the panoply of reasons for and against the impending deed: the reasons that have made Clytemnestra and Orestes into antagonists, and the consequences that may follow from either course of action. Tarrying, here and in the episodes that follow, does not seek to abide in a moment of satisfaction, nor does it heroically bear the weight of fate: it makes visible, and thereby makes disposable, the reasons that converge in a particular moment; it shows that the forces behind this convergence—religion, fate, war, bureaucracies—can be suspended. Rather than turning away from negativity in Bataille's full-throated laughter, Vogl puts on an enigmatic, slightly malicious smile: in the chapters that follow, he seeks out minute yet epochal fissures in the causality of action—moments when not only subjects tarry and transitively open a view on alternatives to their own actions but moments when history itself seems to tarry and render its own fatality questionable. From each of these instances it is clear that the weaker, subjective and intransitive versions of tarrying, like hesitating or dithering, would not be able to convey the full spectrum of meaning.

The history of tarrying that Vogl reconstructs in his careful and focused readings is at the same time speculative and inspiring. It is speculative in a literal sense because it provides us with the image of a world that at each of its pivotal moments could have taken a different direction. And a world in which the speculations of literature and the deeds of historical actors are united by the movement of tarrying inspires, even if only faintly, a modicum of hope.

Note

The translator wishes to thank Patrick Greaney for his invaluable help in revising the translation, and Joel Morris for the translation of the footnotes.

1   G. F. W. Hegel, *Phenomenology of Spirits* (A. V. Miller and J. N. Findlay eds and trans.) (Oxford: Clarendon, 1977), p. 19. The translation 'tarrying with' adopted by Slavoj Žižek, is by Miller; J. B. Baillie has 'dwelling with'; Terry Pinkard will have 'lingering with'.

FIGURE 1. *Moses*, Michaelangelo, c.1515.

CHAPTER ONE
WRATH AND TARRYING

If I begin with an image and with the description of an image, and if in turn I want to describe both together, this complication may perhaps be justified by the fact that nothing, or very little, can be seen in this image. As in many other cases, this image—as well as its description—is generated by an invisibility: or more precisely, it is generated by a gap, by a kind of hyphen, by something that belongs to this image only insofar as it is thoroughly, systematically absent in it. The image in question represents a blank; its description revolves around this blank; and a description of this image and its description cannot but be captivated by the drama of this double omission. This is a case, it seems, of a very special kind of visual puzzle.

That, in any case, is the way in which Freud approached Michelangelo's *Moses* in one of his most beautiful essays: attracted and captivated by a puzzle, by the effectiveness of a puzzle that infects all visible evidence with profound ambivalence. For Freud did not only address himself to this sculpture for the tomb of Pope Giulio II with all possible precautions, with the proviso, for example, that he was not an 'art specialist' but merely an amateur and layman—a proviso

The *Moses* of Michaelangelo

1

that applies equally to the following pages. Rather, he approached the impressive power of this image of the seated Moses at the point where it does not really tell what it is supposed to tell. On the one hand, there does not seem to be any doubt that this Mosaic arrangement—the powerful bearded man with the tablets of the law under his arms (see Figure 1)—somehow refers to episodes from Exodus: for example, when Moses, furnished with the tablets, descends from Mount Sinai, sees the apostate Israelites, their turmoil and their worship of the golden calf, tosses away and breaks the tablets in wrath and finally begins to punish the impious multitude. On the other hand, as Freud remarks, none of this can be gleaned from the statue of Michelangelo: seated, paralyzed, frozen in motion, this Moses is dropped out of the story, comes from nowhere to go nowhere, forever conjoined with the tablets which he does not break.

Freud connects a twofold argument with this Moses, with its image and its narrative. First, he recapitulates the variants of its possible meaning which may accrue to this frozen image in the process of the biblical narrative, and in so doing he marshals the stories provided by contemporaneous art history in its most advanced state to make several claims: that we are confronted with a 'timeless study of character and mood, 'in which a royal priest casts his glance over the fate of 'humanity'; that we can discern a physiognomic study, a 'mixture of wrath, pain, and contempt'; that we can recognize a specific moment in the life of Moses, a dramatic moment, which captures Moses with tensed leg just before his eruption in anger, before he jumps up and metes out punishment, an arrested movement in anticipation of action; finally, that we are dealing with a Moses who is surprised by the tumult of his people, who turns his head slightly to the left, just catching the tumbling tablets, a moment of utmost tension before their fall.[1]

Secondly, however, Freud immediately brackets these interpretations and flips through them only because he presumes they are generated by an absence of any meaning in the conception of the work: 'Has then the master indeed traced such a vague or ambiguous script in the stone, that so many different readings of it are possible?' (215) Against the various attempts at searching for meaning, Freud takes a different path, the path of securing forensic evidence, where only details, trifles, leftovers and refuse, only what is apparently irrelevant counts. A hermeneutics of meaning, which oscillates between biblical story and Renaissance art history, is replaced by conjecture based on evidence which proceeds in the following way.

The first detail, to which Freud dedicates almost four pages of his text, concerns the implication of the index finger of Moses' right hand in the low hanging garland of his beard, which curves from the left side of his face to the right side of his chest. If this detail really has significance, Freud argues, it must lie in its invisibility, in its concealment. It can be explained only as the remainder of a relation, as the trace of a distance covered, as the end point of a movement in which the right hand comes to rest in his beard. And this is Freud's hypothesis and conjecture: initially, Moses sat quietly; he then heard a noise, turned his head, saw some unfolding event, was overcome by wrath, moved his

Storm of Movement

right hand impatiently and energetically toward his beard, became distracted and then retracted—for whatever reason—his hand together with the strand of beard and remained in this new position. What the statue of Michelangelo describes, according to Freud, remains absent: a motion, made and retracted, that manifests itself only from the point of view of its end, as its remainder.

This is where a second detail, a second observation becomes important. Freud claims to notice that Moses' ominous right hand is not only occupied with the beard but also, in a particular way, with the tablets. For these stone tablets not only balance precariously on the seat, turned onto their edge, but it is also unclear what the right hand is doing with them—whether it is supporting them or whether it is being supported by them. Here, too, Freud dares to reconstruct an invisibility to explain and justify this strange manipulation of a sacred object: according to Freud, Moses initially sat upright and carried the tablets like a folder under his arm. The disturbance supervened, his head turned, his left foot prepared to jump up, the hand let the tablets slip and they tilted, held only by the pressure of the arm, until finally the hand moved back to form the 'singularly constrained air of the whole—beard, hand, and tilted tablets'—as a result of a passionate movement of arm and hand, outcome of a reciprocating 'storm of movement' (228). Freud even proposed a flow chart, which retraces a kinetic sequence; he dissolved Michelangelo's sculpture into a series of stills and thereby animated it (see Figure 2): first, Moses at rest; then, the disturbed, irate Moses; finally, the *Moses* of Michelangelo, the remainder of a twitching motion back and forth, hither and thither.

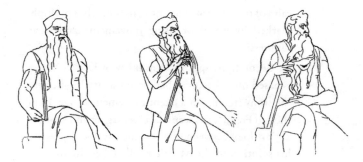

Freud's text, then, consists of several overlays in which biblical text, the statue and the description of the image are held in a peculiar suspension. Despite all his insecurities, his doubts and self-doubts about the figure of Moses, Freud's crime-scene investigation gains the advantages of a doctrine of motion that complicates the relation of narration, image, description and animation in a fundamental way. Against this background we can—with Freud and beyond him—draw a few preliminary conclusions, which will lead to our real topic, 'On Tarrying'.

FIGURE 2. Moses as Movement-Image.

First of all, we must register in Freud's Moses a turn towards the dissolution of narrative and figurative aspects into a diagram of forces, into a constellation that is determined by the effect of opposing forces and their collision. The horizontal 'storm of movement', whose diametrically opposed forces are concentrated in Moses' right hand, is countered by a vertical force field in which the dropping tablets are balanced by the body rising from the left foot. Both are supplemented, Freud says, by the tension between the affective density of the facial expression and the comparative

Forces, Affects . . .

5

calm of the left arm. The entire figure is thus multiply marked by waves of rising movements and their suppression.

Second, the specific invisibility of Freud's Moses is based on a dynamic that manifests itself—behind the stony figure—in a latent movement-image. Even though Freud was a sceptical cinemagoer and avoided any analogy between film and the psychic apparatus, his solution of the Mosaic riddle takes the form of cinematographic analysis. This concerns, first of all, the sequence of those stills that function as images only insofar as they constitute themselves in and through movement and insofar as they have their existence in relation to movement, in a dynamic process to which they owe their emergence and disappearance. Speaking in the Bergsonian language of Gilles Deleuze, this is an indirect representation of time. Freud's graphic reconstruction, therefore, does not show poses or positions in which the sequence of events is symbolically condensed in ecstatic moments; nor does it provide the components that capture—in single images, like the photograms of Marey or Muybridge—a translational motion in space through random, immobile cuts. Freud's phased images, rather, have to be understood as movable cuts, which lead from a quantitative change in space to a qualitative change in time—from the sitting Moses to the wrathful Moses to the *Moses* of Michelangelo. On the one hand, therefore, in Freud's thought experiment, the sequence of movements is divided mechanically into random individual episodes and concerns only the transport of elements through space; on the other hand, these cuts themselves mark the endpoints of executed movements that differ from one another as individual qualities. The entire movement, therefore, comprehends—as duration, as *durée*—the totality of these relations, and is less a changing image than an image of change.[2] Freud's investigation, we can conclude, discovers the hidden qualities of Michelangelo's *Moses* not in this or that meaning but in the real and accomplished movement to which this Moses owes its existence. Freud's 'The Moses of Michelangelo' does not refer to a static image; rather, this Moses becomes a movement-image and represents change in concrete duration, a block of time and space that has become.

The peculiar qualities of this latent movement-image must not be overlooked. For in it, the transition from perception to action is immediately blocked. Between the perception (of the irritation, the noise of the people) and the action (Moses rising from his seat) an interval has opened up in which nothing but arrested movement and blocked action is manifest. With Deleuze, we can see how Freud's 'analysis of the motive forces' (229) approaches the format of an affect-image. It accords with the definition of affect as Deleuze advances it in the tradition of phenomenology. In this tradition, affects mark a rupture in the sensorimotor bond, a cut in the transition from perception to action; they appear in the chasm between confusing perception and delayed reaction. Physiologically speaking, this is a movement impulse, a motor tension in a sensory nerve; ethologically speaking, it has the character of a condition. It is different from a feeling precisely in that it does not determine tendencies univocally, in that it interrupts the chain of motivations from excitation to action. The place of affect is the interruption, its space the interval; in it, the continuation of events is deferred or at least has become questionable. The events to which this Moses refers are determined only in the moment of their indeterminateness. And Freud's presentation itself, in which the affective density of Moses' figure is combined with an arrested 'storm of movement', could be regarded—independently from any cinematic interest—as the first theory of the affect-image.[3]

Thirdly, however, the narrative of Freud's Mosaic arrangement disintegrates into its elements. It breaks free from the continuity, from the sequentiality of any narration and can no longer be integrated into the progress of an epic course of events. This Moses will neither jump up nor not jump up, he will neither hold nor lose the tablets. He has lost his logical place in the narration and interrupts the continuous transition between before and after. He designates the indifference of all action: the either-or of the story is reconfigured by a 'not-only-but-also' and thereby comprises any and all conflicting actions and impulses in the space of their common, non-exclusionary possibility. Freud deciphers in his 'Moses of Michelangelo' a set of signs that cannot be tied to a system of reference: no event, no action, no content, no determined expression, no character and no attribute represent what happens with and through this Moses. This is, rather, a logic of suspension in which the relation between perplexity and the desire to understand is immediately dramatized; in the best of cases it culminates in possibilities, in sheer potential qualities: wrath, indignation, pain, contempt, dignity, pride or eagerness, which will not manifest themselves in this or that action and its continuance and which raise the question whether this Moses has any specific attributes at all: '[. . .] this Moses cannot be supposed to be springing to his feet' (220). Down to its very rhetorical fibre, Freud's text is punctuated by question marks and by active-passive formulae of description. And, in the end, all the qualities and attributes of this Moses exist only in virtual reflexes and connections which have no relationship to real—episodic, historical, traditional, narrative—contexts. Freud's 'Moses of Michelangelo' is a *vir activus*, and the Moses of the Bible is not.

Yet, in the end, this force field, the movement-image, and the unresolved contradictions cannot but assume essential importance, cannot but open a fundamental dimension for Freud which he had alluded to at the beginning of his essay with a short remark on Hamlet. Indeed, Freud says, what is at stake here is the validity of a principle, of the law and of the lawfulness of the law. And this is embodied in a fundamental tarrying. While on the one hand Moses is being carried away to act by his wrath, by his notoriously violent temper, on the other hand the imminent fall of the law effects a turnaround, blocks and inverts the incipient movement. And while in the wrath of Moses—we have to add—the just wrath of the biblical God is continued, the trajectory of this wrath is interrupted and intersected by his law, by the question of its lawfulness. Thus, the law brings the wrath and the action of Moses into a kind of fermata; and thus, inversely, the law is suspended by the incipient action. The wrath that will break the tablets and the law that breaks the wrath motivate and inhibit one another equally.

Law and Tarrying

Of course, we could think here, with Freud, of the structural ambivalence of emotional tendencies that follows from the implication of law and affect and that results in the unresolved coincidence of Yes and No: a hystericized Moses, a Hamlet-Moses that was announced in the *Interpretation of Dreams*, framed by a 'conflict between Id and Super-Ego' that grows and sprawls until 'the ego, unable to carry out its office as mediator, can undertake nothing which is not drawn into the sphere of that conflict'.[4] Above all, however, we are faced with a theory of elementary tarrying and hesitating that brings deed and law, acts and their motivations into a precarious disproportion. This systematically tarrying Moses points to a complex and confusing web of motivations which allows us to identify various elements of an acutely problematic constellation.

Freud himself points out that the text of Exodus itself contains a few inconsistencies in the relation between law and enforcement, between divine and Mosaic intervention. God wants to punish the apostate people (Exod. 32, 7–11), Moses intercedes on behalf of the sinners (32, 11–13), carries out the punishment himself and orders the massacre of his people (32, 31–32) while the entire tribunal at the end is represented as God's own deed (32, 35). These 'incongruities and contradictions' (232) pertain to the diegetic relation between law, transgression and sanction as much as to the authorship of this process; without a doubt, this infects the dubious position of Moses in the unfolding of this biblical narrative of crime and punishment. For on the one hand Moses appears—in Deuteronomy—as the swift executioner of the capital punishment of the secessionists, just as later God's wrath chose in Moses the instrument of execution. In the episode of Israel's dwelling in Shittim it is written: 'So Israel yoked himself to Ba'al of Pe'or. And the anger of the LORD was kindled against Israel; and the LORD said to Moses, "Take all the chiefs of the people and hang them in the sun before the LORD, that the fierce anger of the LORD may turn away from Israel." And Moses said to the judges of Israel, "Every one of you slay his men who have yoked themselves to Ba'al of Pe'or"' (Num. 25).[5] On the other hand, at Mount Sinai, it was not God's punishment that Moses carried out in his wrath. True, he avenges the apostasy from the *lex fundamentalis*, from the newly instituted Decalogue; he sanctions idolatry and the defection from the monopoly of the 'jealous God' (Exod. 20, 5) and repeats in his angry outburst nothing less than the wrath of God. But Freud's reading suggests the possibility of understanding the breaking of the tablets 'symbolically'; as a trope in which Freud claims to detect a cunning transfer of the people's rebellion to the figure of Moses—the breaking of the first and fundamental laws of God.[6] In a curious conjunction, Moses here appears as executioner and usurper, as translator of and impediment to God's will. And this movement seems to culminate in the problematic wrath of the interventionist God of the Hebrew Bible who imposes his law in wrath but also his wrath in the law. This can be understood as unrest within theology, caused by the precarious tension between martial and civil law, between divine omnipotence and justice, and subject to the suspicion of an endless regress, of a core of contingency in divine will.[7]

**Moses
without Bible**

In his early examination of Moses, Freud invested a great deal of energy in the creation of a Moses who acts as interferer and mediator in the divine channels of communication. He blocks the cascade of God's wrath on the way to its realization and does not transmit the law; and, inversely, he counterbalances his own anger with the weight of the law. This is not the traditional Moses of the Mosaic differentiation, the lawgiver who inaugurated the stark difference between the true belief in a single God and the false belief in polytheism, between JHWE and idolatry, who thereby inaugurated a 'counter-religion' against the specialized gods of Egyptian antiquity—an inauguration that left its traces in the history of Jewish and Christian memory and spurred on the escalation of its polemics against paganism.[8] Rather, Freud's 'Moses of Michelangelo' only leads up to this demarcation and touches it, as if to pause before it as if on a threshold: a 'nomotropic' aberrance, a confusion over the question whether and how to position oneself in relation to legality as such.[9]

This peculiar structure of Freud's text can be documented by an additional detail. Freud understands the strange 'horns' of this Moses—in obvious ignorance of their provenance—not as the result of a mistake in translation which made of the transfigured, glowing and radiant face of Moses (*facies coronata*) a horned face (*facies cornuta*). Instead, he concedes the 'animal likeness', the satyr- and Pan-like bestiality, of this Moses whereby he is brought into metonymic proximity to the golden calf.[10] As in Freud's later study 'Moses and Monotheism', in which Moses with the broken tablets presents himself as a retroactive supposition

of a heretical and guilty people, one can already detect
in the earlier text a Moses who is a partial substitute
for the rebellious and idolatrous people. In a certain
sense, this additional component heightens the inner
tension of Freud's figure of Moses and sharpens the
drama at its core. Not only irascibility and law are in
opposition but also the monotheistic imperative and
the turmoil of polytheism; this dubious Moses himself apparently participates, in an unsettling role, in
the apostasy of his people.

Taken together, the diverse problems and tensions
in Freud's conception may help explain why the author
of 'Moses of Michelangelo' obstinately refused to take
into account the visible evidence of Michelangelo's
statue and to relate it to the appropriate passages from
Exodus. Already, in Renaissance commentaries, various
elements—the 'horns' or rays on Moses' head, the cloth
covering his knee, the *blank* tablets under his right
arm—suggested that the reference to this ensemble is
to be found not in the first episode in Sinai with the
golden calf but in the second: when Moses ascends the
mountain a second time with the newly made blank
tablets, beholds God's glory, bears its reflection on his
face, interrupts the proclamation of God's words by
veiling himself and thereby testifies to the renewal of
the covenant. If it is true that Freud with his references
and conjectures was badly mistaken and caused significant confusion;[11] his stubbornness, his misreading,
his misconstructions have to be understood as the
attempt to generate a strictly non-biblical Moses, a
non-testamentary Moses, a Moses who does not function as the translator of God's word, not as the judge
and 'lawgiver' of the Jews and not as an agent of divine

revelation. Rather, we are confronted with a strangely reformed Moses, who suspends The Law, places it in abeyance and interrupts the event of Revelation. Freud's arrested and arresting Moses, who has no relation to the Moses of Exodus, introduces an exemplary blockage into the text of the Bible.

Through this programme of subversion, Freud renders Moses in an almost Paulinian hue. Like Moses, Paul is confronted with the fact that the Jewish people have sinned and rejected the path of salvation. Above all, Paul shares with Freud's Moses a gesture that leads to the suspension of the law. How can the law be suspended? How can the circle of guilt be broken? How can God's wrath and God's justice be balanced? If Paul's project can be understood as a procedure by which the power of the law is pushed towards the margins of its particularity, the *nomos* is subverted and a law without foundation is erected, then the same questions reoccur: how can the original potential of God's wrath be activated and harnessed, how can its insufferableness be justified and moderated at the same time?[12] In his study of Michelangelo's *Moses*, Freud not only presupposed an approximation of Moses to a planned nearby statue of Paul in the tomb of Pope Giulio II; and he not only suggested in his later study on monotheism, as Jacob Taubes has in turn suggested, a Paulinian turn of the problem of Moses.[13] Rather, he opened a Mosaic-Paulinian space of resonance whose tonic is sounded not by the Mosaic and Paulinian event of transfiguration but by the abyss of contingency in God's wrath and law. In this specific correspondence, the Moses of the Hebrew Bible is removed as much from his function of lawgiver as Paul is from the theology of mercy; instead, Freud seems to insist on an insolvability in which neither a Mosaic *sub lege* nor a Paulinian *sub gratia* obtain. A typological relation between Hebrew and Christian Bible is conceived of independently of its testamentary character.

This structural ambiguity in the image of Moses and Paul finally leads to Freud himself. With almost hyperbolic emphasis in the beginning of the text, he recounts the impression that Michelangelo's *Moses* made on him—an effect that figures as the *Urszene*, the original scene of the Moses fantasy, in his exegetical endeavour: Suspense

> [N]o piece of statuary has ever made a stronger impression on me than this. How often I have mounted the steep steps from the unlovely Corso Cavour to the lonely piazza where the deserted church stands, and have essayed to support the angry scorn of the hero's glance! Sometimes I have crept cautiously out of the half-gloom of the interior as though I myself belonged to the mob upon whom his eye is turned—the mob which can hold fast no conviction, which has neither faith nor patience, and which rejoices when it has regained its illusory idols (213).

Freud approaches his Moses from the dark side, from the side of the mob and the apostate people; he sees himself in the position of those who will overturn monotheism, who will break the law and abandon the path to salvation. Even if, later, he adds to this approach the 'disappointment' over the fact that the statue Moses will not 'start up', will not 'dash the tablets to the ground and let fly its wrath' (220), in Freud's scene of approach and observance his own rebellion remains as unatoned as the law remains suspended. Freud, who once confessed to feeling closer in disposition to the historical, biblical, angry and vengeful Moses than to his 'Moses of Michelangelo',[14] carries out a kind of repetition on himself, on the subject of his text, of the contradictory forces and the tarrying of his Moses. This may be the reason for Freud's hesitations about the text; its writing is beset by deep doubts, its publication is delayed and occurs only grudgingly and anonymously, and when it appears he calls it a 'joke', a 'jest', an illegitimate 'love child'. A later corroboration of Freud's hypotheses is published only after a delay of several years under the title 'Supplement to the Essay on the Moses of Michelangelo'.[15] On the one hand, one may understand these gestures as the expression of qualms about a reading that—beyond all art historical, biblical and theological references—is concerned with its own inner coherence and that in this respect has gained the status of a fantasy. On the other hand, Freud's text and its hesitating publication, in which affirmation and withdrawal intersect, seem to repeat the tarrying structure of its subject matter: as if here as well, against the demands of the law and legality, their suspension, the rights of the neurotic and rights of a fantastic, 'hystericized' reading were at stake. From Moses to Paul to Freud, we can read the palimpsest of founding fathers whose authoritative gestures at the same time dispense with the law.

Taken together, these elements compose a system of System of Tarrying tarrying that extends from an aesthetic figure across a context of events into the dimension of principle where it produces a specific suspension: through counterbalancing forces that motivate and block one another; through a movement- and affect-image that creates a moment of indetermination between perception and action; through a dysnarrative function that explodes the syntax of biblical narration; through principles and laws that are brought to the limit of fall and destruction. Paradoxically, we can speak in this context of an energetic inactivity, of a resolute deactivation. Above all, Freud's short text traces a course that leaves behind questions of historical accuracy and produces instead a Moses who transmits no law, succumbs to no affect and who turns to stone in the hither and thither of the tarrying motion. Freud once spoke of the 'tarrying rhythm' of life between order and entropy; here, we could speak of an ethical or ethological tarrying rhythm in which rushing forward and pulling back are constantly superimposed and innervate in the rhythm of their repetition the figure— Freud's figure—of the *Moses* of Michelangelo.[16]

Tarrying is of systematic and fundamental importance here. In contrast to such cognates as indecisiveness, indolence, perplexity, weakness of will or sheer idleness, it is not a stable or instable system of balances; rather, it has metastable properties as it continuously initiates, precipitates and blocks conflicting impulses. A motivational structure is thus installed that undermines the continuity and consequence of sequences of action. Since the biblical plan of salvation knows no tarrying but only delay, Freud's Mosaic

17

arrangement cuts the thread of any redemptive teleology. It touches on its very justification: the figure of repetition internal to tarrying constitutes a circle in which the original act of positing, the wrathful imposition of the law, is enclosed. The activity of this tarrying touches on the contingent foundation of its principle.

Tarrying and its system, therefore, constitutes a relation to the world that is characterized by a specific inner economy, and that includes aesthetic procedures, historical codes, strata of values and epistemological formulae. While tarrying in the Western tradition has always been pushed towards the side of indecisiveness and thus has been disqualified as a frustration of the 'work',[17] it can be recognized as the active gesture of inquiry, in which the work, the action, the execution is comprehended not from the perspective of its enforcement but in the process of its emergence and becoming. Like a lost theme or anathema, tarrying seems to trace a blurred line that comes into precise focus wherever—in a long occidental history—a culture of action and of work is shattered and begins to reflect upon itself. Tarrying accompanies the imperative to act and to work like a shadow, like a ruinous antagonist. One could speak here of a tarrying function: wherever actions and sequences of activities manifest themselves, tarrying marks a hesitation, a pause, a stop, an interruption. An asymmetric relation to time and history is thus installed: insofar as action, according to Nietzsche, proceeds through oblivion and at the same time produces history, the shadow of tarrying fractures this history; it exceeds any historical context in order to conjure up a specific memory: a memory of what has not come to be, a remembrance of a past that never was present, a pre-emptive memory of all those actions and deeds that have not, or not yet, come to pass.

Notes

1 Sigmund Freud. 'The Moses of Michelangelo' in *The Standard Edition of the Complete Psychological Works of Sigmund Freud*, VOL. 13 (James Strachey trans.) (London: Hogarth Press, 1955), pp. 213–19. (Further citations and their page numbers refer to this edition.)

2 Gilles Deleuze sums up his theses on Henri Bergson, in which he discusses the transition between a spatialized, divisible movement to an indivisible duration of movement, with the following equation: 'immobile sections / movement = movement as mobile section / qualitative change'. Gilles Deleuze, *Cinema 1: The Movement-Image* (Minneapolis: University of Minnesota, 1986), pp. 1–11; here, p. 9. See Miriam Schaub, *Gilles Deleuze im Kino. Das Sichtbare und das Sagbare* (Gilles Deleuze in the Cinema. The Visisble and the Sayable) (Munich: Fink, 2003), pp. 89–93. On Freud's ambivalent relationship to the cinema, see Horst Bredekamp, 'Michelangelos Moses als Gedankenfilm: Freuds Ambivalenz gegenueber der Kinematographie' ('Michelangelo's Moses as a Mental Film: Freud's Ambivalence to Cinematography') in Kristina Jaspers and Wolf Unterberger (eds), *Kino im Kopf: Psychologie und Film seit Sigmund Freud* (Cinema in the Head: Psychology and Film since Freud) (Berlin: Bertz und Fischer, 2006), pp. 31–7.

3 Deleuze, *Cinema 1*, pp. 66, 87. Although Freud wanted to keep a distance from the contemporaneous psychological and phenomenological concepts of affect, one can see here that he himself hystericizes the event in

affective moments: the hysterical attack is manifest affect but affect is the 'expression of a general hysteria'. See Sigmund Freud, 'Introductory Lectures on Psycho-Analysis' in *The Standard Edition of the Complete Psychological Works of Sigmund Freud*, VOL. 16, p. 396.

4   Sigmund Freud, 'Inhibitions, Symptoms and Anxiety' in *The Standard Edition of the Complete Psychological Works of Sigmund Freud*, VOL. 20, pp. 77–175; here, p. 118. See Sigmund Freud, 'The Interpretation of Dreams' in *The Standard Edition of the Complete Psychological Works of Sigmund Freud*, VOL. 4, pp. 264–6.

5   Quotations from the *King James Bible*. See Ralf Miggelbrink, *Der Zornige Gott: Die Bedeutung einer anstößigen biblischen Tradition* (The Wrathful God: The Meaning of an Objectionable Tradition) (Darmstadt: Wissenschaftliche Buchgesellschaft, 2002), pp. 152–62.

6   Sigmund Freud, 'Moses and Monotheism' in *The Standard Edition of the Complete Psychological Works of Sigmund Freud*, VOL. 23, p. 48.

7   Peter Sloterdijk, *Rage and Time: A Psychopolitical Investigation* (Mario Wenning trans.) (New York: Columbia University Press, 2010), pp. 98–105.

8   Jan Assmann, *Moses the Egyptian: The Memory of Egypt in Western Monotheism* (Cambridge, MA: Harvard University Press, 1997), pp. 208ff. Friedrich Wilhelm Graf, *Moses Vermächtnis. Über göttliche und menschliche Gesetze* (Moses' Legacy. On Divine and Human Laws) (Munich: C. H. Beck, 2006), p. 48.

9   Eric L. Santner, 'Freud's "Moses" and the Ethics of Nomotropic Desire' in Renata Salecl (ed.), *Sexuation* (Durham, NC: Duke University Press, 2000), pp. 57–105.

10 Freud, 'Moses of Michelangelo', pp. 213 and 215. This mistranslation is apparent in the Vulgate, the Latin translation of the Bible, and can be traced to the ambiguity of the Hebrew word *qeren*, which means both 'ray'

and 'horn'. Freud simply ignores references to this in the literature with which he was familiar. Jewish interpretations have referred to the close associations between the Golden Calf and a 'horned' Moses. See Christoph Dohmen, 'Nuntii Personarum et Rerum. Mose, das leuchtende Antlitz der Tora' ('Nuntii Personarum et Rerum [Ambassadors of Persons and Things]. Moses, the Radiant Face of the Torah'), *Biblica* 86 (2005): 586–7. See also Malcolm MacMillan and Peter J. Swales, 'Observations from the Refuse-Heap: Freud, Michelangelo's Moses, and Psychoanalysis', *American Imago: Studies in Psychoanalysis and Culture* 60(1) (2003): 41–104. Here, p. 79.

11 Macmillan and Swales, 'Observations from the Refuse-Heap'; Franz-Joachim Verspohl, 'Der Moses des Michelangelo', *Städel-Jahrbuch* (13) (1991): 155–76.

12 Jacob Taubes, *The Political Theology of Paul* (Stanford: Stanford University Press, 2004), pp. 23–8, 37, 89–90. Alain Badiou, *Saint Paul: The Foundation of Universalism* (Ray Brassier trans.) (Stanford: Stanford University Press, 2003), pp. 5, 75–85. Sloterdijk, *Rage and Time*, pp. 100–02.

13 Freud, 'The Moses of Michelangelo', p. 220. Taubes, *Political Theology*, p. 90.

14 Ernst Jones, *The Life and Work of Sigmund Freud, Volume 2: The Years of Maturity, 1901–1919* (New York: Basic Books, 1955), p. 367.

15 For the history of the publication of 'The Moses of Michelangelo', see Jones, *The Life and Work of Sigmund Freud*, pp. 363–7, but especially (and with a few corrections of Jones) MacMillan and Swales, 'Observations from the Refuse-Heap', pp. 54–62. A representation of a bearded Moses statuette by Nicolas of Verdun—the basis of his 'Supplement to the Essay on the *Moses* of Michelangelo' (first published in 1927)—was given to Freud by Jones in 1921.

16 See Sigmund Freud, 'Beyond the Pleasure Principle' in *The Standard Edition of the Complete Psychological Works of Sigmund Freud*, VOL. 18, pp. 40–1. Here Freud has moved the neurotic structure and conflict to the level of organic life itself: 'It is as though the life of the organism moved with a vacillating rhythm. One group of instincts rushes forward so as to reach the final aim of life as swiftly as possible; but when a particular stage in the advance has been reached, the other group jerks back to a certain point to make a fresh start and so prolong the journey.' Additionally, it should be recalled that the etymology of the verb 'to tarry' (*zaudern*), which is absolutely related to the verb 'to hesitate' (*zögern*), contains an analogous double movement of the verbs 'to press forward' (*vorwärtsdrängen*) and 'to inhibit' (*hemmen*). See Jacob and Wilhelm Grimm, *Deutsches Wörterbuch* (German Dictionary) (Munich, 1984), VOL. 31, pp. 393ff.; VOL. 32, pp. 22ff.

17 See Michael Gamper's presentation ' "Daß ich meinen Zweck fast ganz und gar vergesse": Unentschlossenheit und Laune als ethische und ästhetische Konzepte der Frühromantik' (' "That I Forget Almost Entirely my Purpose": Indecisiveness and Mood as Ethical and Aesthetic Concepts of Early Romanticism'), *Athenaeum* 9 (1999): 9–38.

CHAPTER TWO

THE RAISED HAND

In the following pages, disparate aspects of a history
of tarrying are assembled in pursuit of the question of
how various procedures of tarrying may be combined
to form a methodology, and how they may coalesce
into a historical and theoretical programme of research,
a programme that investigates rules of conduct with a
view to their implied powers of differentiation. This is
not primarily an investigation of quotidian blockages
and inhibitions, of those micro-dramas and scenarios
that inevitably accompany every artistry of action and
every 'art of action' and that belong to the mastery of
the diversity, of the vital ramifications and decisions
in the process of individual or collective life. Neither
should this result in a collection of the lives and
legends of the great hesitators, which would include
such notables as Fabius Maximus Cunctator, Hamlet,
Büchner's Danton and the Zeno Cosinis of the twentieth century. If, instead, the outlines of a function of
tarrying are drawn and a gesture of radical tarrying is
delineated, it is to describe a constellation in the strict
sense of the word: a constellation of situations and
circumstances which become significant because in
them action and its relation to the world have become

23

problematic. Tarrying condenses a critical, crisis-focused relation of deed and inhibition, of action and reason, of law and execution; by necessity, this will churn up the ground on which a world, and a relation to that world, is constituted.

We surely can still appreciate the freshness of an initial deed in the ways in which Greek tragedy has transferred modes of action from the gods to the mortals. Tragedy seems to have been searching among the mortals for vessels capable of containing the power of this transference, of interrupting the course of divine fate with the appropriation of secular competencies for action. Even though the deed was always too immense for the tragic protagonists and always exceeded their strength, even though they escaped fate only at the price of their own downfall, a scene was thus opened that exposed the intricacies of actions in such a way that their fatality became questionable. Already the architecture of Greek theatres provided a facilitating *dispositif* or apparatus: not only because in it the course of the developing action presented itself to the fixating and judging gaze of the audience but also on a purely technical level: the stage or *skene* interrupted the race-course (*dromos*) in the oval of the theatre and created a detached space for separate action (drama)—a space that allowed for entries and exits and, therefore, for a 'sheering out of the infinite loop of competition'. For the staging of the *Oresteia* in 485 BC, part of the theatre's space was separated, the closed circle dissected and thus the conditions created for the reciprocal attention of focused spectator and emplaced action.[1] Theatre and drama have constituted themselves from their inception as space-time wrested from the gods, as demonstratively interrupted action.

This theatrical constellation focuses our attention on a first, incisive scene of tarrying which demands extensive commentary because it is presented as both unimposing and potent: unimposing, because it is quickly surpassed and overwhelmed by the ensuing action; potent, because it arises from a disastrous history and leads to a complicated aftermath. It is a short scene in the *Oresteia*, one of the first great dramatic cycles in European literature; it occurs in the middle of the trilogy, in *Choephori* (*Libation Bearers*), which follows *Agamemnon* and leads into *Eumenides*.

The scene rests in the centre of a fatal complication, in the middle of a matrix of actions that reaches far beyond the story of the drama and encompasses mortals, gods and demigods—actions raging across time and space, cascades of deeds and crimes that generate more deeds and crimes. The fate of the Atreides and the action of the *Oresteia* pushes up against the margins of this short scene: Agamemnon is already dead, slain by his wife Clytemnestra and his cousin Aegisthus; both now reside as rulers at the court in Argos. At the beginning of *Libation Bearers*, Orestes, son of Agamemnon and Clytemnestra, wants to follow Apollo's oracle and avenge the murder of his father. With a ruse, he enters the palace undiscovered, is received and immediately proceeds to act. He kills Aegisthus, steps outside the palace, meets his mother, who only now recognizes her son, and is, at the moment when his hand is raised and poised for the blow, interrupted, arrested in the execution of his act. All of this is condensed in a question that Orestes now asks. After Clytemnestra uncovers her breast and asks her son not to strike at the mother who once nourished

Orestes

him ('Easy, my son, take pity on this breast, child, / that you so often, half-asleep, would suck / with soft gums for the milk that let you grow!'), he hesitates and asks himself, or rather his silent accomplice Pylades: 'What should I do [*ti draso*], my Pylades; How can I kill my mother?'[2] Even if in the end this leaving-off does not happen, even if Orestes is reminded, with the only words Pylades utters in the entire drama, of the oracle of Apollo, of its fulfilment, of the possible wrath of the gods and thus is propelled to act; even if here a 'turning point'[3] is reached and brief tarrying will immediately pass into bloody deed, an unresolved questionability remains. A dramatic tarrying before a dramatic act.

This short scene is critical and striking because it interrupts, for a short moment, the reproduction of fated, fatal events, a murderous contagion and the dark fate of the Atreides. It is critical because this inhibition manifests doubt about a sequence of events, about the way of its unfolding. On the one hand, the continuation of the action and the strike against Clytemnestra follow the edict of the Apollinian oracle and transfer Orestes' deed back into the hands of the gods. On the other hand, the short flash of Orestes' question causes unrest in the play, an annoyance and a syncope in its programme: mother and son have hurried towards one another in the intention to kill one another and meet, at least for a moment, in the stillness of a fundamental abeyance, marked by Orestes' 'What should I do?' With his tarrying, Orestes has not only become lonely and singular but also for a brief moment, as Pylades remarks, an offence to Providence, an obstruction to divine rule and the carrying out of its demands.

The question's special quality consists in the fact that it does not only defer Orestes' deed but also that it presents the deed for a moment in the aspect of its sheer potentiality. A gap is thus opened in which the deed appears as contingent, that is, as neither necessary nor impossible, at a threshold on which action and inaction are joined without contradiction and where the orientation of action becomes blurred. Put in Aristotelian terms, tarrying at that moment marks a potentiality, if potentiality—as Giorgio Agamben has shown in Aristotle's *De anima* and *Metaphysics*—is a capacity for incapacity, a capacity not to be or not to act. The capacity for language, for example, implies the capacity to be silent; the capacity to think the capacity not to think; and the capacity to see the capacity to be blind. Potentiality, *dynamis*, cannot simply be understood as the opposite of actuality, *energeia*. Rather, it eludes the logical form of affirmation and negation and produces and leads—as potentiality—to a state of suspension that remains present in every actualization and realization. In the ninth book of *Metaphysics*, Aristotle says: '[...] everything that potentially can subsist cannot be actualized. That which is potential can both be and not be; the same thing is at the same time capable of being and of not being.'[4] Capacity or potentiality, therefore, does not only imply the ability to do or be this or that but the power not to actualize, not to transit into actuality. Capacity is in intimate relation to incapacity and inserts the existence of not-being into existence; it does this in such a way that the capacity of not-being is included and conserved in the actuality of being. Capacity does not abide in sheer privation or in non-actuality but keeps potentiality present in actual being or acting. That is why the short utterance of Orestes is so exemplary and significant: to the dramatic necessity of his action it adds a sense of contingency that can no longer be forgotten; it adds the potency of a 'not' in which the not-wanting, the not being able to, the not-execution of the deed is preserved. Perhaps this contingency is another name for the tragic dynamics with which the deed is actualized in Aeschylus' drama.

Phantom of a Deed

A second aspect is important: Orestes' tarrying generates the phantom of a deed—the imminent matricide—the singularity of which consists precisely in the fact that it is embedded in a complex and far-reaching network of references. It refers to past actions and anticipates future sequences and, therefore, renders visible conditions and conditions of conditions. Not by accident does Aeschylus' text surround Orestes' question with a dialogue between Orestes and Clytemnestra, a stichomythic dialogue which in rapid alternation treats the questionability of the action, its provenance and perspectives; 20 lines, in which the problematic of this tragedy, its complications, its motivations, its catenation of actions and consequences are exposed, exchanged and examined. Orestes' tarrying is explicated in opposing roles, in an arresting assault of positions and counter-positions, of arguments and counter-arguments, which have approximately the following structure: You want to kill your mother (asks Clytemnestra)? Did she not kill father and husband (asks Orestes)? Did he not violate mother and family by sacrificing Iphigenia (this is the counter-question)? Was this not done with sufficient reason and in war (this returns the question)? And so forth: Will not the avenging spirits follow the deed? Will they not also follow if vengeance is neglected and murder una-toned? Was not the killing of Agamemnon a conse-quence of fate? Will not fate be accomplished in the present deed? Will the matricide not draw the curses of his relatives? Are these relatives not cursed them-selves? Here is Aeschylus' dialogue:

CLYTEMNESTRA. I bore you, reared you. Let me grow old with you!

ORESTES. What! Kill my father, then make your home with me?

CLYTEMNESTRA. Fate had a role to play in this, my son.

ORESTES. If so, then your death, too, is no less fated.

CLYTEMNESTRA. Aren't you afraid, child, of a mother's curse?

ORESTES. No, you gave birth to me, then threw me out to suffer.

CLYTEMNESTRA. How so when I had sent you to a friend's house?

ORESTES. Son of a free man, I was sold, disgraced.

CLYTEMNESTRA. If so, then where's the price I got for you?

ORESTES. I'm ashamed to taunt you openly with that.

CLYTEMNESTRA. Go on, but name your father's lusts as well.

ORESTES. Don't you dare judge him: he suffered, you sat at home.

CLYTEMNESTRA. A woman suffers, kept from her man, my son.

ORESTES. But it's hard work that keeps her safe at home.

CLYTEMNESTRA. You seem, child, bent on murder-ing your mother.

ORESTES. No, you'll be murdering yourself, not I.

CLYTEMNESTRA. Watch out for the mad dogs of a mother's curse!

ORESTES. What about my father's, if I don't do this?

CLYTEMNESTRA. I'm singing my own dirge to a deaf tomb!

ORESTES. Yes, my father's fate is bringing you your death.

CLYTEMNESTRA. Ah, you are a snake I bore and suckled! (140–1)

All past and future events are called forth in their interconnection and represented in their *epoché*: in an arrested and retained time, in which the temporality of the vast network of actions in the *Oresteia*, its pasts and futures are collected. Tarrying, however brief, reveals itself as a process of progressive determination which the executed deed does not conclude but only interrupts. The phantom of action not only leads to the questionability, to the problematic reason of a future deed; it also presents an intensity of negotiation that manifests itself in the turmoil and the back-and-forth of arguments. One is reminded here of the turmoil that precedes the murder of Caesar in Shakespeare: 'Between the acting of a dreadful thing / And the first motion, all the interim is / Like a phantasma, or a hideous dream: / The Genius and the mortal instruments / Are then in council; and the state of man, / Like to a little kingdom, suffers then / The nature of an insurrection.'[5] Such is the turmoil and the insurrection, the discord, the in-between time and the epoch, in which tarrying produces a phantom deed; an endless negotiation and a continuing process of determination.

Finally—and this would be a third aspect, a third char- acteristic—the prospect that this brief scene opens up is all the more difficult and consequential as it con- founds the criteria of any action. What is opposed in Orestes and Clytemnestra are not only two perpetra- tors, or a culprit and a victim, but rather two actors who legitimize their actions in different ways. On Clytemnestra's side—as has been repeatedly pointed out—there is the archaic right of matriarchy, the ques- tion of blood relations, the system of blood feuds, the matrilinear descent. Visible on Orestes' side is a differ- ent orientation, which rests on the importance of pat- ricide, the institutions of the monarchy and institution in general: a patrilinear discourse that finds support in Apollo's oracle. At the heart of tarrying and of the question of tarrying are not only different motifs and reasons for or against a deed; rather, what is at stake are different principles and systems of valuation—differ- ent encodings of the social and moral world.

A process of differentiation is thus initiated, a progressive distinction that cannot immediately pass into decision, into judgement. This is suggested by the formal question 'what should I do?' and the choice of verb, *dran*. For this verb selects and accentuates a spe- cific aspect of action. While the verb *prattein* is focused on a goal and the accomplishment of an action, and while *poiein* has to do with the work on an object, with producing and making, Aeschylus' use of *ti draso* and *dran*—in the sense of 'to commit something', 'wanting to do something'—opens a dimension in which the activity of the act is itself in play. This *dran*, from which the name 'drama' derives, relativizes the importance of the actor and refers neither to a goal-oriented process nor to a 'consecutive chain of necessarily connected and unified effects' but to the 'decisive point' at the beginning of an action. Bruno Snell has insisted that *dran* in Aeschylus' *Oresteia* is always related 'to the overcoming of tarrying and indecisiveness' and that it marks beginnings and the decisions to act. Even if Snell's radical translation of *dran* as 'to decide' has been criticized, it undoubtedly connotes that vestibule of acting in which the decision and the inception of an action are themselves put into question.[6] The interrogative form, inherent in the verb *dran*, comes to a head in the 'what should I do?', in the *ti draso* of Orestes. The joining of the dramatic action is dissolved; it disintegrates into single, problematic and tense situations in which a reversal or a detour of the action is imminent or at least not impossible. As much as *Libation Bearers* is itself characterized by a movement of 'tarrying and swaying', the antagonism between the 'propelling and the inhibiting forces' culminates in Orestes' question.[7] The drama of action— or the action in a drama—is inhibited and brought to reflect on its own inhibition. Orestes' tarrying may contain a madness of decision, an eccentric moment in which not only the deed but also the world in which it is to be realized are suspended. Tarrying touches on the joints and sutures that keep this world together, or not: it is a crisis in the conception of the world and its order, a crisis of the system of judgement.

Court of Law   Through this tarrying a problematic constellation comes into view that persists throughout the further development of the *Oresteia*. Already at the end of *Libation Bearers*, Orestes is persecuted by the vision of avenging spirits, by the Erinyes or 'dogs' of his mother, and everything that his deed was supposed to solve and dissolve—the reproduction of guilt and injustice—again becomes an open question. Where does the rage of misfortune find its end, the last sentence of the drama asks, where might there be rest? This problem and this problematic structure reach far into the last drama, into *Eumenides*. Here, at the end of the trilogy, the reciprocal regeneration of vengeance and counter-vengeance and the antagonistic universe of the Atreides is arrested and, in a surprisingly untragic fashion, determined and clarified in a kind of trial; the *skene* is transformed into a trial scene, action into a transaction. Orestes, still persecuted by the Erinyes and still supported by Apollo, is acquitted after a lengthy hearing of both parties in the temple of Pallas Athena on the acropolis of Athens, and the Erinyes are reconciled. Yet this procedure only repeats the aporetic situation that was first opened up by the scene of tarrying. The vote among the elected judges results in a draw, which in any case was caused by the partisan vote cast by Athena for Orestes—a draw and an aporia that can result in an acquittal for Orestes only by way of procedural measures. In the end, not only the gods that are involved—like Apollo or Athena—are reduced to being parties in a suit; even the ultimate solution is nothing but the derivation of a fundamental undecidability.

This activates the paradoxical presupposition of the judgement. For in the trial of *Eumenides* it is not only the guilt or innocence of Orestes that is at stake; a kind of meta-trial takes place, in which justice judges justice and injustice. Even if a verdict is rendered, even if Orestes is acquitted and withdrawn from the vengeance of the Erinyes, this comes about through a decision between undecidables, through the fact that the antagonism between two contrary principles of justice becomes a dispute in which one of the parties is necessarily wronged. Archaic matriarchy is abolished through patriarchy in favour of patriarchy—a fact that prompted Franz Grillparzer to see in this trial a 'masterpiece of partiality and injustice'.[8] The decision, therefore, was a different decision before the decision; it was legitimized—against the backdrop of the reformation of the Greek justice system in the middle of the fifth century BC—through proceedings in which lawmaking was the result of jurisdiction. For this reason, the Erinyes could not be placated and pacified by the trial but only through the *peitho* of Athena, through the magic force of her word, through seduction and persuasion. The decision of what is undecidable has persisted as an implacable remainder in the new institution of the court of law and its judgements; it conserves for memory—in the first court scene of Western theatre—that in every decision that which is defeated remains as a scar. What is problematic and aporetic thus persists until the end. On the one hand, the trial scene with its arrest of the action repeats the pause with which Orestes' tarrying dramatized the action. On the other hand, the decision at the end of the *Oresteia* reproduces the tarrying, problematic structure of the deed and with this correspondence marks the fissure that runs through the cosmos of antiquity.

The Problematic If we gather all these aspects of tarrying—the interruption; the potentialization of the deed; the phantom of the deed; undecidability; and the overthrow of systems of judgement—then we can draw a twofold conclusion. Tarrying can be understood as a poetic procedure that enacts in dramatic fashion the destitution, the suspension of dramatic action. This tarrying and its question ('what should I do?') cannot be subsumed without any remainder under the categories of dramatic or performative acts; rather, it stages a decisive inactivity. Its appearance, the interruption and the pause of the action, marks an ellipsis that accompanies all dramatic action, reduces it to zero and submits its power of imposition to examination. This tarrying is neither an activity nor an inactivity; rather, it indicates a moment in which the components, the conditions, and the implications of action are gathered, in which a deed is manifest not in its execution but in its inception. In this sense, the stichomythiae inserted into the interplay of speech acts suspend their activity and transformation in the dramatic space. This is a dramatization in the most literal sense, in which the drama, the *dran*, exposes itself and the questionability of its presuppositions and procedures. Orestes' tarrying, which for a moment defers his deed and transforms it into a mere possibility, subtracts action from its implementation and execution; it should be understood as a pseudo-act that interrupts not only the syntagma of action but also renders the dramatic act inactive: as a transitory suspension that undoes all concurring maxims, principles and laws. Hölderlin would have called this poetic aspect of tarrying a 'caesura', a counter-rhythmic interruption, an objection to the rhythm, an inactivity, which deactivates the act. This null stops the 'onrushing change of representations' in order to gather between the before and after their totality, their 'highest point', their sheer potentiality.[9]

Second, however, the system of tarrying gains in this way in subliminal efficacy and justifies the claim that tragic questions and problems, condensed in the phantom of the deed, persist with their answers and solutions in interrogative form. Orestes' tarrying encapsulates a problematic structure which no deed, no dramatic solution can resolve, neutralize, compensate or eliminate; it traces out a fissure that runs across all interlocking events and actions and indicates their joints and interfaces. It produces an infinite singularization of the act. In contrast to the raised hand attributed to Plato, who, it is said, interrupted himself at the point of striking a disobedient slave and thereby controlled, mastered and punished his anger[10]—in contrast, that is, to the motivated prevention of an act, the raised and suspended arm of Orestes does not bring about any solution. Tarrying, we could say, is a programme that searches for the unsolved questions and problems behind given solutions and answers. In tarrying, the tragic hero is not only lost in the labyrinth of his actions and their consequences; he is also exposed to the urging of a violent questioning, to a problematic being that persists, disguised and deferred, in all instances of its dramatic solution. His tarrying produces the phantom of a deed that in the turmoil of conflicting arguments preserves an anomic core that intervenes even in the negotiations of the court. The solution at the end has not resolved Orestes' tarrying, it has only enveloped it.

Notes

1 Cornelia Vismann, 'Das Drama des Entscheidens' ('The Drama of Decision') in Cornelia Vissman and Thomas Weitin (eds), *Urteilen/Entscheiden* (Judging/Deciding) (Munich: Wilhelm Fink, 2006), pp. 94–5.

2 Aeschylus, *The Oresteia* (Alan Shapiro and Peter Burian trans) (Oxford: Oxford University Press, 2003), pp. 139–40. (Further citations and page numbers refer to this edition.)

3 Hermann Josef Dirksen, *Die aischyleische Gestalt des Orest und ihre Bedeutung für die Eumeniden* (The Aeschylean Figure of Orestes and its Meaning for the Eumenides) (Nuremberg: H. Carl, 1965), p. 113. See also Theodore Ziolkowski, *Hesitant Heroes: Private Inhibition, Cultural Crisis* (Ithaca: Cornell University Press, 2004), p. 34ff.

4 Artistotle, *Metaphysics*, 1050b, 10. Quoted in *Aristotle: Metaphysics* (Richard Hope trans.) (Ann Arbor: University of Michigan Press, 1960), p. 195. Giorgio Agamben stresses this argument in *Potentialities: Collected Essays in Philosophy* (Daniel Heller-Roazen trans.) (Stanford: Stanford University Press, 1999), pp. 177–84.

5 William Shakespeare, *The Tragedy of Julius Caesar*, II.i.62–9. Quoted from *The Riverside Shakespeare, Second Edition* (Boston and New York: Houghton Mifflin, 1997).

6 On this, see Bruno Snell, *Aischylos und das Handeln im Drama* (Aeschylus and Action in Drama) (Leipzig: Dietrich, 1928), pp. 10–19. On the discussion of this problem of translation, see Vismann, 'Drama des Entscheidens': 96.

7 Snell, *Aischylos*, pp. 127–32.

8 Franz Grillparzer, *Sämtliche Werke* (Complete Works) (Moritz Necker ed.), VOL. 14 (Leipzig: Hesse, 1903), pp. 152.

On the irreconcilable relationship between dispute and litigation, see Jean-Francoise Lyotard, *The Differend: Phases in Dispute* (Georges van den Abbeele trans.) (Minneapolis: University of Minnesota Press, 1988). On the 'undecidable' in the decision, see Michael Niehaus, 'Die Entscheidung vorbereiten' ('To Prepare the Decision') in Vismann and Weitin, *Urteilen/ Ent-scheiden*, pp. 17–36. Apollo provides the critical argument of paternal law in the case, with recourse to which Anaxagoras negates the mother's roll in procreation and, as evidence, also cites the birth of Athena from the head of Zeus. The Furies' demand for vengeance is thereby biologically delegitimized. See also Christian Meier, *The Political Art of Greek Tragedy* (Andrew Webber trans.) (Baltimore: Johns Hopkins University Press, 1993), pp. 105–12.

9   Friedrich Hölderlin, 'Remarks on "Oedipus"' in *Friedrich Hölderlin: Essays and Letters on Theory* (Thomas Pfau trans. and ed.) (New York: State University of New York Press, 1988), p. 102. See Werner Hamacher, 'Afformativ, Streik' ('Affirmative, Strike') in Christiaan L. Hart Nibbrig (ed.), *Was heißt 'Darstellung'?* (What Does 'Representation' Mean?) (Frankfurt: Suhrkamp, 1994), pp. 341–71.

10 Seneca, among others, describes this episode and its stoic turn. When asked by a friend who happened by what he was doing in that strange position, Plato supposedly answered, 'I'm exacting punishment from an angry man.' See Seneca, 'On Anger, Book 3' in *Dialogues and Essays* (John Davie trans.) (Oxford: Oxford University Press, 2007), pp. 28–9.

CHAPTER THREE

A WALLENSTEIN-PROBLEM

The pragmatic aspect of tarrying lies in deactivation, its aesthetic dimension in the caesura and its meaning in interrogative power; it marks the precarious margin in the inception of a deed, an interval that continues until the deed is eventuated and pushed onto the stage of time and space *as* an event. It holds the event back until the moment in which this push occurs. Tarrying, therefore, can be understood as a remainder of eventuality in the event, as a latent and insistent reservation within that which is being done and suffered, that which manifests itself and actually happens. It continues to refer to a critical point and to a turnover in which the structure of tarrying resolves itself and passes over into the economy of incidents, into the sequence of events. It is, therefore, to be expected that the function of tarrying plays a special role in that kind of knowledge of events that since the end of the eighteenth century is called by the collective singular 'history', in that type of investigation that concerns itself with the temporality and phenomenality of events as such. If the eventuality of events refers both to the inception of an occurrence and to its

Knowledge
of Events

representation, its entrance and its perception, then it must move to the centre of reflection of a new, modern conception of history: insofar as this conception comprises the convergence of occurrence and representation, of incidence and meaning, of story and history, thereby doubling the inscription in the real with the real of writing.[1]

If the tarrying of tragic heroes revealed an intensity of negotiation at the moment of acting, then the question of tarrying reflects a system of occurrences the factual and theoretical unlocking of which constitutes the epoch of history. Tarrying—such is the thesis—discloses the state and the quality of historical eventuality, it reveals how history becomes the discourse of occurrences. The function of tarrying has a historical dimension. In the context of attempts in which the last decades of the eighteenth century sought to discuss 'a priori history'[2] or the a priori of history, this question could be called a Wallenstein-problem. For Schiller's drama *Wallenstein* was not only occasioned by a historiographical question, by the question of how becoming turns into having become, of how 'blind vagueness' turns into a coherent whole within the order of discourse;[3] *Wallenstein* does not only lead to that point where the poetological investment of history and the historical substrate of literature converge and enter into negotiation. Rather, in the transition from Schiller's historical treatise on the Thirty Years' War to the Wallenstein trilogy, the being of historical events, their formation and their complex internal structure on the threshold to the nineteenth century are at stake; all of which, it seems, becomes urgent in the notorious tarrying and hesitating of which Schiller's merchant of war, that erratic, dramatic and tragic figure, has been accused since its inception.

While in his historical treatise Schiller speaks simply of the 'idleness' of Wallenstein—who, after the death of Gustav Adolf, King of Sweden, and after the decimation of the Catholic troops, no longer intervenes in the war; who withdraws in 1633 to his camp in Bohemia and keeps still between two fronts; who does not do anything; who engages in unclear negotiations and becomes 'a secret equally unintelligible to friend and foe'[4]—the Wallenstein of the drama has an even more drastic profile. He pursues a politics of deferral, waits for outstanding occasions or constellations, keeps open various options and avenues and finally appears as an enigma of whom it remains unclear whether he harbours secret intentions, whether he vacillates between different possibilities for action or whether he simply does not know what or whether he can want. All this, in order to miss, in a last, brief, tarrying the last chance to act. In the middle play of Schiller's trilogy, the *Piccolomini*, these antidromous tendencies are staged—one that moves toward resolution, decision, intervention and deed, another that, in the figure of the opaque condottiere, undermines and prevents exactly that. How is this to be understood? In what way can we speak of a system of tarrying in Wallenstein's case? And what can we learn about the formation of historical events?

Hesitation and Power

First, and in a very preliminary way, Wallenstein's strange pausing reveals a strategic option, which coincides with a historical practice of military and political power. The legendary Quintus Fabius Maximus

Cunctator comes to mind, the Roman general who, as Plutarch and Livy recount, exhausted Hannibal's troops and in particular his elephants by evasion and stalling, by means of a 'Fabian' strategy of which it was said that 'hesitation had restored the state.'[5] Furthermore, we can recognize here the first outlines of a new art of governing, which, at the latest since the seventeenth century, is no longer based solely on *potestas*, on the sovereignty of a ruling power, but on *potentia*, on the attempt to measure the durability of political power according to its potential to gather possibilities and to accumulate the wealth of land, people and goods. This speaks of a fluidity of a form of power that maintains itself in its suspension and no longer intervenes immediately in the here and now. Already, the historical figure Albrecht Wenzel Eusebius von Wallenstein had operated in the shadow of emerging bureaucratic states, had recognized the power of a standing army and the importance of economic infrastructures and had pursued with his military might a strategy of avoiding the confrontation of battle; Schiller's baroque general can be understood as the incarnation of a new political rationality which realizes itself in the management of potentialities and excels in the handling of faculties and possibilities. From everyone, the play states, 'he extracts the proper energy' and knows how to make the 'faculties' of others his own.[6] Wallenstein, who at times was called a man of possibilities, in this respect is the prelude to the modern programme of a political power that manifests itself in its reticence, in indirect government, in excess and in the exercise of potentialities.

All of this, however, does not do justice to Schiller's strange dramatic figure. Schiller's dramatic architecture lays out the gradual formation of an event and its critical moments. The trilogy's construction itself opens various perspectives on this event. The first play, *Wallenstein's Camp*, represents the raw reality of war in which what happens, happens; in *Wallenstein's Death*, at the end of the trilogy, everything revolves around realization, around the *kairos*, around missing or capturing the right moment; the middle section, *The Piccolomini*, opens up a space in which the halting action maintains a balance between the possibility of events and their realization. Wallenstein's tarrying is prepared by a strategy of deferral that minimizes all existing relations, relaxes the bonds of war, translates all activity into the subjunctive mode and compiles nothing but incompatibilities. This is a first and essential aspect that characterizes not this or that Wallenstein but an impossible agent and, with him, a liquidation of the state of the world.

There is, in the middle of the trilogy, a loyal Wallenstein who still supports the Catholic emperor in Vienna. Then there is a Wallenstein who revolts against the emperor and plots treason against the empire. There is one who pretends to negotiate with the Swedes, and another who really negotiates with them. There is a Wallenstein who seeks reconciliation between the Swedish troops and the troops of the Emperor, and a Wallenstein who plots against both. One Wallenstein only pursues plans for his own principality; at the same time, another pursues a policy of religious tolerance, of unifying Europe, of a new realm of peace or simply of

Wallensteins

a German Empire free of foreign occupiers. Whether Wallenstein will resign his generalship, will anticipate the actions of the court or perhaps betray it, will build an army, will accept conditions, forge new treaties or maintain his neutrality—we are, at the end of this perusal, confronted with a fantastic Wallenstein who constantly deviates from himself, whose attributes never converge and whose programme culminates in a 'I prefer not to.' Although the conditions of future actions have become ambivalent, this is not a case of fundamental doubt, of hesitating and tarrying in the face of multiple political and military options. Rather, Wallenstein is confronted with a choice to the second degree in which not the choice between different options is demanded but the choice of a choice, the choice between choosing and not choosing. The difference emerges between someone who only chooses and someone who knows he has to choose; the existence of someone who has no choice is no longer possible: 'I cannot say as yet what I will do' (77). Wallenstein's tarrying has assumed fundamental proportions and touches on the problem of a will that has lost its principle and that progresses from multiple choices to the will for nothing to, finally, the nothing of the will.

Since all actions and all actors are transported into a historical subjunctive, Wallenstein's programme leads straight into a hell of possibilities. This provokes reminiscences of a prominent example, the theatre of multiplicity that Leibniz designed for the end of his *Theodicy*. Leibniz' ending is not only a philosophical dialogue that, based on a story by Lorenzo Valla, encapsulates a series of episodes and narratives: the question posed by Sextus Tarquinius to Apollo's oracle, the encounter between Sextus and Jupiter in the presence of the priest Theodorus, Theodorus' question to Jupiter, who refers him to Pallas Athena, his journey to Athens and his dream of a gigantic pyramid and the 'Palace of the Lottery of Life'. The subject of the story is, rather, the mode and status of what can be represented as an event at all. A dream of the contingency and variability of events: in this dream, Theodorus is led into the various rooms of the immense palace, and there he sees not only different interiors but different and new worlds. He sees the Sextus who does not heed the oracle's advice, does not go to Rome but to Corinth where he dies as a 'wealthy, beloved, and respected man'; in another room, he sees the Sextus who reaches Thracia where he marries the king's daughter, remains childless and ascends to the throne; and he sees at the apex of the pyramid the chamber of the real world, in which the real Sextus has made yet another decision: he has left the temple in anger, disdained the counsel of the gods, gone to Rome, wreaked havoc, raped Lucretia, the wife of his friend, and lived out his life 'expelled, beaten, unhappy.'

In each tract of this architecture of events is a Sextus who carries a number on his forehead and who acts out, 'like in a theater play,' a variation on his life. From a single moment—when Sextus leaves Apollo's temple—this dream represents the infinite series of versions of the same event that opens up from the apex of reality to the base of an infinite pyramid; it shows 'a regular sequence of worlds [. . .], that only contains the case in question and changes its circumstances and consequences.' A simple event—the story of Sextus

Tarquinius from the moment of Apollo's oracle—is thus captured in the contingency of its reality and made infinite in two ways: first, through its immersion in an infinitely divisible and ramified world in which the sequence of events can be divided into ever smaller incidents, suggesting a infinitesimal expansion of possible narratives; second, through the multiplication of the interpolated events, each of which forms the apex of its own, infinite pyramid of alternate possibilities.[7]

Leibniz, with this pyramidal structure of events and worlds, introduced an original representation of the problem of contingent futures and revealed a specific perspective on the modern format of events. Every event contains a bifurcation at which it disperses into different modifications, variants and versions and represents itself as an inner multiplicity. The event appears as a diagram of diverging lines of eventuality. However Leibniz might have justified the selection of the real world from the catalogue of its possibilities, his narrative must be understood as a momentous model of the architecture and ontology of the historical world. If it is true that every event in the world is also possible differently; if it is true that everything that happens is determinable and therefore necessary but also one variant from the reservoir of possibilities, then the obsequious and the angry Sextus, the satisfied and the unhappy Sextus are equally possible but not possible together, not 'compossible'. They are possible only in strictly separate worlds which themselves are 'incompossible'—not possible in the same time and space. On the one hand, not everything possible is, for Leibniz, possible in every possible world; the contingency of world events opens up a space that comprises many 'possible worlds' but not a 'world of all possibilities'. The multiplicity of possible worlds—which are not possible together—filters chaos and limits chance: God, as it were, rejoices in the sacrifice of unborn or half-born things, beings and worlds. On the other hand, Leibniz shows how the given world is constituted against the horizon of its possible modifications; he shows how modern thinking of contingency posits the reality of the real world as the first condition of its possibility.

Wallenstein's tarrying in Schiller's play leads to this point of indecision. In tarrying, in the arrested moment of choice between choosing and not choosing, the event articulates itself as bifurcation and presents itself in its quality as diagram of diverging series. The event as point has been distended into an erratic surface; Schiller's stagnating Wallenstein bursts into various Wallensteins that form a catalogue of possible worlds in which events are perhaps possible but not possible together, and, as incompossible events, have not yet happened, may have happened or never will happen. The event here is the expectation of the event; an unborn world of histories that remains enclosed like a crypt within the real, historical world.

This Wallenstein programme, therefore, contains a reservoir of incompossible elements; it effects a de-creation of the world, indicates a hesitation before its birth and thus breaks from the chronological order. The character of potentiality can be represented neither in temporal sequence nor in epic or dramatic succession; it dissolves linear arrangements of before and after. Linearity deltas into an infinite ramification of

Aeon

47

possibilities, all of which seem to be equally true or equally likely. A simultaneity of incompossible presents emerges like the shadow of all the possibilities of that which actually occurs. This happens in an a-chronic time, in which the past, the present and the future are simultaneously present, a time in which the past continues but in which 'tomorrow' also 'roams today' (238). More precisely: time has an a-topical structure. For just as the infinitesimal, infinitely divisible moment never happens now but instead has already or has not yet occurred and thereby holds in suspense what has happened and will happen from the river of time, so too the time of the *aeon* emerges from *chronos*. This time of the event encloses an empty time without present, which frees itself from all actual, physical content and contains only what has happened or will happen but which at the moment has not happened, no longer happens or has not yet happened. The intervention of this in-between-time in Schiller's Wallenstein has been remarked upon;[8] with Gilles Deleuze and Félix Guattari, one could say that this in-between-time in the event is always

> a dead time; it is there where nothing takes place, an infinite awaiting that is already infinitely past, awaiting and in reserve. This dead time does not come after what happens; it coexists with the instant or time of the accident, but as the immensity of the empty time in which we see it as still to come and as having already happened.[9]

While in the actual present nothing really happens, the virtual character of events dissolves the chronology of actions.

There are, fundamentally, at least three different times or time-structures in Schiller's *Wallenstein* that reflect the complex structure of the event. There is, first, passing, chronological time which concerns the sequence of events and the random collision of active and passive bodies, and which operates in the background of the drama as the raw fatality of the war. To this joint time of incidents and sequences of action, there is contrasted, second, a 'kairological' time, the time of the *kairos* that infects with increasing urgency Wallenstein's notorious 'temporizing', his deferrals and delays, and that manifests itself in the drama of the not-yet and the 'too late' (153). Both times shape the dimensions of action in the drama, its measured, delayed or precipitous pace. Against these two times, a saturnine, a-chronic time intervenes in the tarrying of Wallenstein; more precisely, a time of the *aeon* that transforms the present into imminent futures and pasts, and frees itself of all present content. In this empty dimension of time, the event (in)exists in its multifariousness, in its variants and versions; in it, all deeds, incidents and characteristics are bracketed and pluralized—they form the time of the historical subjunctive.

Wallenstein's ominous obsession with astrology is not at all a belief in fate or in the astral determination of events. Rather, it expresses the complex relation between time forms. The path of chronological and cosmological time is related to constellations, to the quest for a moment that needs to be captured. Together they are not led by the stars to information on what should or could be done but, on the contrary, as Goethe noted, to a fundamental dearth of interpretation: to the confusion of the past, the present and the future, which suspends all possible action as well as the sequence of time.[10] The result is not only an aesthetic freezing of time but an extension of the field of conditions, circumstances and complications in which the temporal core and the ontology of an event is, so to speak, cracked open. The *plurale tantum* of 'history' corresponds in this temporal structure with an *eventum tantum*, with the collective singular of an event that still is missing its historical place, its location in time-space, its becoming and its entry into the world.

Process of Determination

Hegel, in an early review, once defined the Wallenstein situation as 'one-sidedness of indetermination amidst nothing but determinations', as the one-sidedness 'of independence amidst nothing but dependencies', and saw in it the fissure in tragic action, the 'submission of indeterminacy to determinacy' and, finally, a mistaken realization, a monstrosity and a failed theodicy: 'When the drama is over, everything is over, and the realm of Nothing has triumphed; it does not end as a theodicy.'[11] This is not quite correct and misses part of the specific process of realization in Schiller's drama. Schiller himself summarized the situation more poignantly as a specific quality of the aesthetic state of mind. In the twenty-first of *Letters on Aesthetic Education*, Schiller distinguishes between two forms of indeterminacy or 'determinability': an 'indeterminacy from lack' as an 'empty infinity'; and an 'aesthetic freedom of determination', an indeterminacy from excess as 'full infinity'. The first can be determined because it is not determined at all, because it is limitless, passive and without reality. The second, however, can be determined because it is not exclusively determined, that is, it can comprise all possible determinations without choosing or favouring a specific one; it is limitless because it is infinitely determined—a state of 'heightened reality'. In the space-time realm of appearances, this state functions as interruption, as gap, as 'null', Schiller says, because it invalidates every determined effect and annuls every limit. It has the tendency to arrest the change of times and to expand, as a-chronic duration, 'into a larger surface'. At the same time, this state is dynamic, active and mobile in a particular way in itself. In contrast to the state of empty indeterminacy, the aesthetic state of active determinability consists of a constant positing and retracting, a making and destroying of determinations; a throng of possibilities and an internal oscillation, in which every determination is arrested and blocked by the next one. The result is an internal rhythm of tarrying determinations, a dynamic opposition of forces. The deployment of the 'entire faculty' here is tantamount to a tarrying that in the inception of a decision, before the transition to the deed, culminates in a certain intolerability.[12]

This is the situation in which Wallenstein's strategy of deferral transforms itself into tarrying and misses, at the beginning of *Wallenstein's Death*, the opportunity, the favourable constellation for action. In Schiller's vocabulary, this is the 'pregnant moment', a critical, precise and over-determined moment. In it, the reservoir of possible Wallensteins is confronted with the necessities of the phenomenal world and allows for the choice, the selection of events to happen, however arbitrary they may be. In the words of *Wallenstein*:

'When a decision should be made, so much / Depends on luck and how things come together— / And individually and scattered do / The threads of fate appear, those moments that / Are brought together only at *one* time / In life, there to create a nodal point' (75). In the pregnant moment, a thoroughly determined representation is completed and characterized by 'the absolute definitiveness of the subject';[13] in this respect, Schiller stages a drama of determination. Already the Wallenstein in the *History of the Thirty Years' War* was characterized by contradictory determinations as a traitor and as a bringer of peace; in the Wallenstein trilogy, the determinations have multiplied and transformed contradictoriness and ambivalence into a character without character, the result not of privation but of a process of over-determination.

Vice-Diction   This Wallenstein is always non-identical with himself, and constitutes himself not through negation or contradiction but through a procedure of determination that Deleuze, with reference to Leibniz, has called a 'vice-diction'. The virtual agent thus generated differs from the actor later realized—the traitor—not through contradiction but through a process of infinite differentiation. 'Vice-diction' is the procedure of tarrying: it accumulates attributes and determinations, compares them, determines them reciprocally and suspends them; it runs through a multitude of possible Wallensteins; it produces a differential Wallenstein always at odds with himself; it attempts the complete determination of the Wallenstein problem.[14] What Goethe called Wallenstein's 'fantastic existence', his 'fantastic spirit', is the vessel of all characteristics and attributes whose spectrum, in hyperbolic condensation, comprises 'the grand and ideal' as well as the mad and the criminal, without centre, without support: deliberate and improvisational, ambitious and resigned, true and traitorous, angry and loving, brusque and conciliatory, obsessed with power and placable, sovereign and dependent, clever and betrayed at the same time.... The vacillating 'character image'[15] has dissolved all attributes from an identical bearer and generated a characterless character, a suspended excess of determinations: a Wallenstein that is not undetermined but infinitely determined. At the same time, the progressive determination discloses the historical constellation and their conditions under which an individual and limited Wallenstein will realize himself.

The over-determined and the limited Wallensteins coincide only in infinity, and yet they lead to the point where the Wallenstein event emerges. After all, Schiller focused all dramatic attention on the fact that nothing but a simple circumstance, a 'lucky' or 'unlucky chance' (133) will prompt the selection of events and initiate the realization of occurrences. Not this or that decision but the capture of the messenger Sesina at the beginning of *Wallenstein's Tod* marks the point of crystallization, the metabolic and pregnant moment when the pent-up power of decision discharges into events and leads to a solution: from sheer 'capability' or 'faculty' is initiated an entire network of activity with its own laws. This is the moment when the fantastic Wallenstein will have become the real Wallenstein, that is, a traitor. Schiller lets Wallenstein himself describe his situation: 'The *world* is *narrow* but the mind is *vast*. / Thoughts can exist so easily together, /

But objects in a space will soon collide. / The place *one* fills is taken by *another*' (152). With regard to the philosophy of history, it is hard to overlook that this mixture of tarrying, chance and realization represents a lessening or weakening of the principle of sufficient reason, or at least a questioning of this principle which, according to Leibniz, excludes all spontaneity, concedes no accidents and presupposes a causal inclination for everything that happens. Schiller has dramatized this doubt repeatedly; for example, in the tarrying gesture with which Elizabeth consigns Mary Stuart's death sentence to the administration, in the doubling of her declared will with a shadowy non-will, in the way she lets bureaucratic circumstances hasten the decision and in the referential confusion that obscures in whose name the execution actually happened.[16]

Drama of Origination
Wallenstein's tarrying, therefore, comprises a complex relation of determinations and determinability and can be described as the critical arch in which the 'entire faculty', the infinite determinability collides with finite determinations and characterizes, if you will, a self-overwhelming of experience. Tarrying addresses both the complexity of the situation and the contingency of its solution and keeps both, situation and solution, in suspension.[17] It follows a method of complication which extends to the comprehension of problems and their conditions at the same time as it traces a line to the ontology of history and reveals the complex inner structure of the event. Strictly speaking, the event consists of these two different parts or temporalities which belong together and yet are absolutely dissimilar. On one side is what happens, what occurs, what is done and suffered, what is embodied in things and

relations: the catenation of incidents and the world of spatio-temporal accidents. Yet on the other side is something that is not represented in data and circumstances and that does not disappear in its realization: the gathering of an a-chronic time beyond the happenings of the present; the opening of an empty time in which different qualities, attributes and activities coexist simultaneously and without contradiction. The present, which passes as a mobile moment of now and concerns active and passive bodies, transcends itself, moving towards an a-chronia that contains the event in its unresolved multiplicity. Schiller's historical drama is characterized by a mania for realization—he once speaks of the 'necessity behind events' (87)—that is forcefully checked and arrested and that is condensed in Wallenstein's tarrying: in a pronounced desire for non-actuality. Thus the world of events is doubled by an inchoate world, an emerging world. Unsettled possibilities, blocked determinations, incompossible elements and suspended attributes—all this not only characterizes an unborn world but also the way in which the event unfolds in the moments of its genesis. The infinite determination, the problem, belongs to the order of the event. Wallenstein's tarrying activates a drama of emergence that unfolds on two levels: on the level of virtual attributes, infinite determinateness and progressive descriptions of problems; and on the level of real solutions, where all possible actors, actions and incidents are pushed onstage and dressed in their definitive masks, costumes and roles.[18]

Schiller, understood as a prominent representative and theoretician of historical sense, allows us to see the

History and Contingency

correspondence of history and aesthetics, of historical and literary discourse. More importantly, however, in this correspondence, in this transformation of historical into literary figure a programme is delineated that conjoins the representation of history with the irrevocable contingency of events. Schiller's discourse understands history from the point of view of the temporality of change, gravitates towards the shattering of form and pursues a catharsis of historical interconnections. In this respect, Wallenstein's tarrying is neither a theatrical device nor simply the idiosyncrasy of a particular character; rather, it has exemplary, systematic value. What happens here, on Schiller's stage, has hyperbolic dimensions and short-circuits every realization with a counter-realization. According to Schiller, the reality of events does not conform to the type 'Wallenstein betrays the Empire,' but is, instead, surrounded on all sides by possibilities and ramifications of this Wallenstein-event. Wallenstein appears as a tremulous silhouette and as caught in a kind of permanent revision. Unfinished variants flow around the event like a haze—'the haze of the unhistorical', as Nietzsche would have said[19]—that is no less real but less actual. We assist not only at the formation of an event but at the event of a formation that is not absorbed into an actual form. In the nineteenth century, at the latest, historical time itself falls into a rhythm of tarrying and unfolds in a motion that—like the motion of spring and escapement in a watch—does not unwind continuously but through hesitating and tarrying.[20] With good reason, Schiller's Wallenstein drama has been recognized as an 'entire historical world' that appears 'not only more philosophical than philosophy itself but also more historical than history.'[21] Schiller's arrangement measured the void inside the collective singular 'history' and reclaimed the cohesion of history and becoming, history and genesis. Wallenstein's tarrying leaves behind the sprawl of its variants; and it offers, to summarize, an elemental, primary scene for the contingency of the historical world.

Notes

1   Reinhart Koselleck, *Futures Past: On the Semantics of Historical Time* (Keith Tribe trans.) (Cambridge and London: MIT Press, 1985), pp. 27–38, 103–04, 106.

2   Letter from Goethe to Schiller, 24 January 1798, in *Correspondence between Schiller and Goethe, From 1794 to 1805, Volume 2: 1798–1805* (L. Dora Schmitz trans.) (London: George Bell and Sons, 1879), p. 23.

3   Friedrich Schiller, 'Was heißt und zu welchem Ende studiert man Universalgeschichte? Eine akademische Antrittsrede' ('What Is, and To What End Do We Study Universal History? An Inaugural Lecture') in *Sämtliche Werke* (Collected Works) (V. Gerhard Fricke and Herbert G. Göpfert eds), VOL. 4 (Munich: Carl Hanser, 1958), pp. 761–5.

4   Friedrich Schiller, *The History of the Thirty Years' War in Germany* (Rev. A. J. W. Morrison trans.) (Boston: Francis A. Niccolls & Company, 1901), p. 334.

5   From the famous verses of Quintus Ennius: 'Unus homo nobis cunctando restituit rem'. On the Roman historiography about Fabius Maximus, see Regina Rieck, *Die Darstellung des Q. Fabius Maximus Cuncator und des M. Claudius Marcellus in Livius' dritter Dekade* (The Representation of Q. Fabius Maximus Cunctator and of M. Claudius Marcellus in Livy's Third Decade)

(Dissertation, Techn. Universitaet, Berlin, 1996); Paul Erdkamp, 'Polybius, Livy and the "Fabian Strategy"' in *Ancient Society* 23 (1992): 127–47. And on the unsoundness of the legendary strategy, see Hans Beck, 'Quintus Fabius Maximus—Musterkarriere ohne Zögern' (Quintus Fabius Maximus—Exemplary Career without Hesitation) in Karl-Joachim Hölkeskamp and Elke Stein-Hölkeskamp (eds), *Von Romulus zu Augustus: Große Gestalten der römischen Republik* (From Romulus to Augustus: Important Figures in the Roman Republic) (Munich: C. H. Beck, 2000).

6   Friedrich Schiller, *Wallenstein* (Jeanne Willson trans.) in Walter Hinderer (ed.), *Wallenstein and Mary Stuart* (New York: Continuum, 1991), p. 59. (Further citations and page numbers refer to this edition.)

7   Gottfried Wilhelm Leibniz, *Theodicy: Essays on the Goodness of God, the Freedom of Man, and the Origin of Evil* (E. M. Huggard trans.) (La Salle, Illinois: Open Court, 1985), pp. 284ff.

8   See especially Jeffrey Barnouw, '"Das Problem der Aktion" und *Wallenstein*' ('The Problem of Action' and Wallenstein) in *Jahrbuch der deutschen Schillergesellschaft* 16 (1972): 330–408, here, pp. 369ff. Dieter Borchmeyer, *Macht und Melancholie: Schillers 'Wallenstein'* (Power and Melancholia: Schiller's 'Wallenstein') (Frankfurt: Athenäum, 1998), pp. 50ff.

9   Gilles Deleuze and Felix Guattarri, *What is Philosophy?* (Hugh Tomlinson and Graham Burchell trans) (New York: Columbia University Press, 1994), p. 158. Gilles Deleuze, *The Logic of Sense* (Mark Lester trans., with Charles Stivale) (New York: Columbia University Press, 1990), pp. 162–8.

10 Johann Wolfgang von Goethe, 'Die Piccolomini: Wallensteins Erster Teil. Ein Schauspiel in fünf Aufzügen von Schiller' ('The Piccolomini: Wallenstein, Part One. A Drama in Five Acts by Schiller') in *Sämtliche Werke*

(Collected Works), VOL. 6.2 (Munich: Carl Hanser, 1988), p. 684.

11 Georg Wilhelm Friedrich Hegel, 'Über Wallenstein' ('On Wallenstein') in *Werke* (Works), VOL. 1 (Eva Moldenhauer ed.) (Frankfurt: Suhrkamp, 1986), p. 619.

12 Friedrich Schiller, *On the Aesthetic Education of Man* (Elizabeth M. Wilkinson and L. A. Willoughby trans) (Oxford: Oxford University Press, 1967), pp. 145–9, 141. See also Horst Turk, 'Die Kunst des Augenblicks. Zu Schillers Wallenstein' ('The Art of the Moment. On Schiller's Wallenstein') in *Augenblick und Zeitpunkt: Studien zur Zeitstruktur und Zeitmetaphorik in Kunst und Wissenschaften* (Moment and Point in Time: Studies on Temporal Structure and Metaphorics in Art and the Sciences) (Christian W. Thomsen and Hans Höllunder eds) (Darmstadt: Wissenschaftliche Buchgesellschaft, 1984), pp. 306–24.

13 Schiller to Goethe, 15 September 1797, in *Correspondence between Schiller and Goethe, From 1794 to 1805, Volume 1: 1794–1797* (L. Dora Schmitz trans.) (London: George Bell and Sons, 1877), p. 400. This corresponds directly to Lessing's 'fruitful moment' from *Laocoön*, which distinguishes itself through the 'free play' of imagination. See Gotthold Ephraim Lessing, *Laocoön: An Essay on the Limits of Painting and Poetry* (Edward Allen McCormick trans.) (Baltimore: Johns Hopkins University Press, 1984), p. 19.

14 See Gilles Deleuze, *Difference and Repetition* (Paul Patton trans.) (New York: Columbia University Press, 1994), pp. 189–90.

15 Goethe, 'Die Piccolomini', pp. 670–91, especially p. 689.

16 Friedrich Schiller, *Mary Stuart* (Charles E. Passage trans.) in Hinderer, *Wallenstein and Mary Stuart*, pp. 368–70, 391–3.

17 See Turk, 'Die Kunst des Augenblicks', p. 318.

18 See also Deleuze, *Difference and Repetition*, p. 190. When Deleuze speaks of two faces or sides of ideal events—of love that searches for the progressive determination and the linking of ideal joint fields, and of one that is sudden or angry and realizes itself in condensations or discharges—so too can we think of the two directions of Piccolomini, present not only in Mars and Venus but in also Max and Octavio Piccolomini: the face of love and the face of betrayal and outrage.

19 Friedrich Nietzsche, 'On the Uses and Disadvantages of Philosophy for Life' in *Untimely Meditations* (R. J. Hollingdale trans.) (Cambridge: Cambridge University Press, 1997), pp. 63–4. See Deleuze and Guattari, *What is Philosophy?*, pp. 96–7.

20 One of the great tarriers of historical drama, Grillparzer's Rudolf II, formulated such a policy of movement. The historical subject, he says, should learn, 'That in a clock in which the spring impels / A counter-wheel must regulate the course / Or else the movement might straight-off run down / And not with measured speed strike out the time' ('an der Uhr, in der die Feder drängt, / Das Kronrad wesentlich mit seiner Hemmung, / Damit nicht abrollt eines Zuges das Werk / Und sie mit ihrem Zögern weist die Stunde'). Translation quoted in Franz Grillparzer, *Family Strife in Hapsburg: Tragedy in Five Acts* (Arthur Burkhard trans.) (Yarmouth Port, MA: The Register Press, 1940), p. 123. See Franz Grillparzer, 'Ein Bruderzwist in Habsburg: Trauerspiel in fünf Akten' in *Sämtliche Werke* (Complete Works), VOL. 9 (August Sauer ed.) (Stuttgart: Cotta, 1887), p. 108.

21 Wilhelm Dilthey, *Von deutscher Dichtung* (On German Poetry) (Leipzig and Berlin: B. G. Teubner, 1933), p. 411.

CHAPTER FOUR

A DOCTRINE OF METHODS

Our reflections so far have attempted to comprehend tarrying as a gathering spot for questions concerning the nature of decisions and events that accompany the occidental culture of the deed, and that contain a variety of pragmatic, aesthetic and historical components and perspectives. Tarrying interrupts sequences of action and functions as a caesura; it potentializes action, leads into a zone of indeterminateness between Yes and No, exposes irreducibly problematic structures and opens an in-between-time in which the contingency of incidents can articulate itself. Tarrying, such is one conclusion, operates near the interfaces, the joints, the synapses and the hinges where the coherence of world situations is determined, or, more precisely, where the aggregate state of this world, its solidity and its progression, is at stake.

Finally, tarrying reveals an attitude, a composure of and in the world that in the nineteenth and twentieth centuries has undergone radical changes, and fits into a peculiarly split image. On the one hand, the diagnosis of modernity after all the social, political and industrial revolutions has revealed a kind of action based on the notion of a system, an implemental mode

Pathologies of the Will

that links actions and consequences without considering the role of the individual, that selects options, orients events and instals a social mechanism and a frenetic and functioning society determined by action and production. Sovereign tarrying—like the tarrying of the sovereign—is a thing of the past; acting is organized by functional systems and unburdens the individual's culture of activity. On the other hand, a new kind of man seems to be born from this change; he stands next to the active, liberated, 'free-acting' and interested actor and presents himself as a strange *homo cunctans* or *cunctator*. These questions do not entirely belong to the domain of social engineers, who, since the nineteenth century, have registered a correlation between the increase of mechanical, material, physical, physiological and psychological work and the growing amount of fatigue, neurasthenia and exhaustion—a malfunction of the machine. Rather, the textbooks of pathology have become increasingly concerned with distortions, anomalies and paradoxes of the will. A growing number of publications on phenomena such as somnambulism, trance-like states, hypnosis and automatism—believed to play a complex role in individual and collective action—is accompanied by observations that relate specific inhibitions and blockages to 'pathological indecisiveness.' Examples can be found in the annals of psychiatry: a patient who for hours sits in front of a jacket or a glass of water before he can reach for it; a well-known author who capitulates before the last lines of his work and never manages to publish it; a notary who, despite multiple attempts, is unable to place his hand on a prepared document to notarize it: 'he was incapable of using the

quill'; a wealthy gentleman who stops in the middle of
the street and does not move again . . .[1]

An extreme example of this can be seen in cases of
chronic 'dependence on doubt and brooding' (*folie du
doute, manie de foullier*), in which a 'state of continuous
tarrying' is combined with 'trifling motives', loses itself
in endless questioning and never reaches a conclusion.
There was, for example,

> [a] mentally very alert woman who could not
> walk on the street without asking herself this
> question: What if someone jumps from a win-
> dow and lands right in front of me? Will it be a
> man or a woman? Will they be injured or dead?
> Will they suffer head or leg injuries? Will there
> be a pool of blood on the sidewalk? How will I
> recognize that the person is dead? Should I call
> for help or flee the scene or say a prayer? Will I
> be accused of having caused the accident? Will
> I be able to prove my innocence? . . .[2]

There are other cases, like that of a young 'law stu-
dent' and a young and successful merchant who are
haunted by an 'anankasm in the form of a question' or
by a 'morbid sense of precision', who are subject to a
'mania for reasons' and who constantly run through
all possible questions, who 'burrow into ever greater
detail', get caught in a 'labyrinth of problems' without
issue, poring over 'questions of creation', of Nature, of
the cosmos, of man; their thought processes 'arise in
an unconsciously motivated brooding about the reasons for perfectly simple phenomena, in a rumination
that seeks to penetrate its object beyond all limits of
reason and is, therefore, doubtful about the reality of
objective phenomena.'[3]

If the decisiveness of the will is characterized by the tendency to arrive at a final state, to provide a stable foundation for the ego, to choose a manifest motivation and to affirm or negate a work or a deed,[4] then the above-mentioned pathologies indicate precarious states in which the unwanted is done; the 'I will' does not result in a willing; willing itself impedes what is wanted and the anticipation of consequences suspends any action, resulting in an infinite regress of reasons and causes. This is, at the same time, a 'theoretical' and a 'theorizing' passion in which the transition to practice no longer functions: it is as if the principle of sufficient reason had developed some kind of demonic attraction and infected all thinking with an infinite failure. Within the field of systemic action (or acting systems), modern psychiatry discovers enclaves, black holes and blanks in which all action breaks off, hesitates or simply collapses—a pathology of the will that extends from simple apathy to paralysis of the will to a will that blocks itself. A peculiar chiasm of social systems emerges: the more systemic action is divorced from the reasoning and the impulses of individuals, the more motivation, cause and reason for acting become individual problems.

Man without Qualities It is all the more remarkable that the pathologies of the will begin to structure a discourse that has to be called 'literary'. This is not only manifest in the many literary figures, from Melville's Bartleby to Valéry's Monsieur Teste, whom Robert Walser once called 'true titans' of tarrying, and Wolfgang Koeppen 'knights of the tottering form';[5] figures who emerge from a kind of drunkenness of the will, who refuse with increased effort to be or do anything—whatever it may be—or who seem to believe that the 'very idea of ending no longer has any meaning in a mind that knows itself well enough.'[6] This is not just a literary phenomenon; it is also a more general sounding, a programme of exploration, a gesture of questioning which gains in methodological and systematic coherence. Tarrying and its pauses becomes the operational base of a discourse: tarrying generates an analytical method inside literature.

Robert Musil's enormous project, for example, opens with the narrative invention of a protagonist who has taken 'a holiday from life'.[7] This is not a version of the contemplative life but, rather, a system of tarrying which is highlighted by the fact that this man without qualities first appears with all sorts of qualities, with a surplus of qualities, so that the man without qualities represents qualities without man; he is equidistant to all qualities and therefore hesitates at the limit of their realization. Resisting 'determinate occupations', 'single-minded will' and 'specifically directed drives' (273), he has reached a threshold at which action has become as difficult as inaction and a decisive course of life can neither be affirmed nor denied. This former soldier, engineer, mathematician could be a saint or a pilgrim, an adventurer or a criminal, a poet or simply someone who is disappointed, and he could claim for each a separate approach to the world. But Musil's Ulrich is and does all of this at the same time, and, confronted with a choice, even with the choice between choosing and not choosing, he remains stranded in the antechamber of all choices. This hesitation amounts to tarrying, to a relation between determination and determinability, and thus to the formation of an aesthetic existence: Ulrich 'hesitates in trying to make something of himself' (269); then he felt that 'a man longing to do something with all his heart does not know whether he should do it or leave it undone' (274). And with some effort he finally slides into a hypothetical life, into the uncomfortable situation of someone who somehow 'constantly seems to be poised in the act of creation' (266).

Insufficient Reason

At the base of this career of becoming a 'potential man' (270) is a double tarrying, one originary and one derived therefrom. For already in a youthful essay on patriotism—written as a pupil at the aristocratic Theresianische Ritterakademie—he had had the audacious insight that no love of one's country can guarantee that one finds the best of all possible countries, and that God himself preferred to talk about his creation in the 'subjunctive of possibility': 'God creates the world and thinks while He is at it that it just as well could be done differently.' Not surprisingly, the school officials' ensuing investigation could not decide if this essay constituted an act of calumny against the fatherland or blasphemy against God (14). The scandal, both for divine government and the administration of the Empire, is once again a fundamental doubt about the principle of sufficient reason.

To repeat, then: the formulation of this principle since Leibniz is designed to create an asymmetry between all possible worlds so that a hesitation or a tarrying of God regarding their choice may be excluded. That anything happens at all is reason enough to presume in all events a logic of preference that favours one among all possible varieties. And because something happens, there is no accidental randomness, nothing that would be equally possible: if one were equally possible as the other and therefore indifferent, nothing would have happened or been created. Here is Leibniz' formulation of the principle: 'In nature there is a reason why something exists rather than not "just as there must be a reason why this exists rather than that". Laplace later provided the following version: 'Actual events have a relation to their predecessors based on the obvious principle that nothing can come into being without a cause that generates it. Under the name "principle of sufficient reason," this axiom refers even to the most insignificant actions.'[8] Insofar as it is certain that not everything that is possible can equally exist, the sufficient reason for all incidents and their causes remains external to their sequence and must consist in God's primary choice, who chooses the existing world from the possible worlds according to its measure of perfection. And God always chooses the best.

The God of Ulrich's youth, however, was obviously indifferent to the choice of worlds A, B or X; or rather, he was befallen by a numinous tarrying in his creativity. The juvenile essay not only attacked the divine or imperial decision for the best of all possible worlds or fatherlands and proposed a ruinous principle of indifference for which everything is indifferent. It had, more pointedly, installed in an audacious inversion the Principle of Insufficient Reason as the essential axiom to explain why anything happens in the world at all: inversion of theodicy. The 35th chapter of the first volume of the *Man without Qualities* explains: just as one cannot know what 'true' patriotism, 'true' Austria or 'true' progress is, so too are all these qualities void of reason, foundation and content; and yet these un-reasons are driving forces 'on the point of realization' (141).

This is especially clear in the ominous 'parallel action' in Musil's novel. Even if it is completely unclear what it is about, what its reasons are and where it is supposed to lead, it can be understood as prominent case of an event that precedes its causes and that, in a kind of hysteron-proteron, will one day have produced its own reasons. Not the best reasons but missing reasons bring this world into existence; and precisely this world relation is baptized 'Kakanien' by Musil. Reasonlessness is its principle, its measure is 'muddling through' (329), and the cacophony of its mode of being lets it appear in the eyes of that distant god in a historical subjunctive.

Dark Theodicy

If what happens to a thing, what it suffers or does is called—according to Leibniz—an event, then we have to conclude that the sufficient reason is that which contains as one of its predicates the event: the concept of a 'thing'. Sufficient reason is the identity of event and predicate in a concept; as concept, it functions like a signature or term, gives a foundation in nature to every predication, and finds its logical formulation in the implication of the predicate in the subject.[9] Precisely in this respect, the world of the empire in 1913 can only appear as lacking a reason, and lacking a concept; as much as might happen in it, it contains events only at the price of an elementary elimination or subtraction of predications: 'The new cure for syphilis was making . . . Research into plant metabolism was moving . . . The conquest of the South Pole seemed . . . Professor Steinach's experiments with monkey glands were arousing . . . Half the details could be left out without making much difference' (390). These ellipses turn the principle of sufficient reason into a principle of indifference and with its additive, paratactical sequence give a logical form to the statement 'this or that happens'. They do not converge in any reason. The world and its history have fallen, on the eve of the Great War, into a rhythm of tarrying; they have lost their decisiveness and any semblance of a foundation. They bring forth a dark theodicy that—perhaps—one day will give birth to a, or THE event, along with its reasons.

The realm of events and the realm of reasons have separated and let the created world appear to be entirely anti-Leibnizian in the form of a 'prestabilized disharmony' (1207). This is no longer the baroque multiplicity of possible worlds but the finite world of possibilities. Here, all bifurcations, divergences, incompossibilities, and disharmonies belong to the same world, to the same throw of dice: 'The play of the world has changed markedly in modernity, as it has become a play that diverges from itself;' and the divergent series leave in one and the same world bifurcating, incompossible traces—incompatibilities that in the moment of the event do not exclude or even contradict one another.[10]

This is neither the work of a sinister deceiver god nor the effect of a mysterious abyss: rather—to put it briefly—this disharmonious and groundless world results from a dispassionate form of observation, which Musil's novel calls 'statistical'. The order in which probability calculus and statistics since the end of the nineteenth century have brought the sequence of events consists in a specific unmooring of incidents and reasons, of events and causality. A statistical norm emerges when the frequency of events is first separated from its motivations and then each incident left to occur in this or in that way. From this perspective, Musil's novel shows, the law of average, normal distribution and probability allow all possible events to also result in an opposite outcome and still preserve an overall direction and tendency. Upon this gesture rests the 'axiom' of probability calculus. And if one wants to reconstruct a certain 'path of the world' from it, this conclusion is permitted: 'it would not be different from what it is, if all were left to chance' (1207).

Statistics   That is also what the founders of social and moral statistics had said: whatever an individual does or does not do for whatever reasons, nothing changes the overall course of events, which is coherent only insofar as it ignores individual reasons and responsibilities. Already in 1832, the statistician Alphonse Quételet said:

> The regularity with which each year the same crimes are committed and are met with the same punishment in exactly the same ratio is one of the most significant facts the statistics of the courts teaches us [. . .] Miserable state of the human race! We can count in advance how many will soil their hands with the blood of their neighbors, how

> many counterfeiters, how many poisoners
> there will be, almost as if one can predict
> how many births and deaths there will be.
> Society contains within itself all the crimes
> that will be committed. In a certain sense, it
> is society that commits them, and the crim-
> inal is only its tool.[11]

No matter how accurate and consequential this remark
may be, it points to the fact that a new ontology of
accidents now determines the ontology of events; it
severs their realizations from their causes, and offsets
those events that occur with those that occur differently or not at all. The events in the novel, which make
up the history of the Austrian Empire, happen this
way or that, are neither real nor unreal, are only to a
certain degree, with a certain probability, in the world.

　　This is the place where the 'incoherence of the
world' and the 'indecisiveness of the individual' (787),
the Empire and Ulrich meet. The cosmos of statistical
probabilities called Austria has brought forth a
strangely impersonal life, a life of lower density or
viscosity, a double life in which intentions and events,
individual volition and regularity, particular and
universal motions rarely if ever meet—'it's as if we had
two destinies—one that's all superficial bustle, which
takes life over, and one that's motionless and meaningful, which we never find out about' (786). The
tarrying of the man without qualities repeats the tarrying rhythm of an unconceivable Austrian world and
its stochastic mass of events, a world that exists at the
margins of its unborn possibilities. 'But the possible
includes not only the fantasies of people with weak
nerves but also the as yet unawakened intentions of

God' (11). With its ground receding into the slumbering intentions of God, this world turns into a *mundus fabulosus*, just as Leibniz' pupil Christian Wolff understood the real world to change into a fabulous world once the principle of sufficient reason no longer applied.[12] The realm of incontrovertible reasons is doubled by a realm of parabolas that produces imaginary relations 'in a dream' (647), and that nonetheless is situated within the historical world of the pre-war period. Against this background, Musil's novel develops a double programme: on the one hand, there is the concern with the possibility of a well-motivated life and the moment of decision, guided by the principle of induction—a concern whose narrative and theoretical fate we will leave aside. For, on the other hand, there is the question of what doctrine of method the procedure of tarrying implies. If the existence of the world of the Empire was determined by the principle of insufficient reason, then its analysis adopts a method that Musil simply calls 'fantastical exactitude'.

Fantastic Exactitude   One particular case exemplifies the essentials of this method as they apply to the analytical discourse of novel as a whole: the case of Moosbrugger the (sex) murderer that takes place in the uncomfortable zone between health and idiocy, between responsibility and its absence. On the one hand—as the famous 62nd chapter of the novel's first volume states—this case is subsumed by a logic that supplies for each case a rule, follows the rule with a judgement, joins the judgement with a decision and thereby guarantees the continuation of activities and events. This is the path of the 'pedantic exactitude' of the courts that, in Musil's words, identifies the case with long-held and 'two-thousand year-old legal concepts' (267), never hesitates and executes its will with a univocal and goal-oriented sense of order. Pedantic exactitude is never at a loss for reason or thoroughness.

On the other hand, the question arises about what kind of fact is constituted by Moosbrugger's deed. Moosbrugger himself, during his ill-fated attempt at representing himself, had posed this question and thereby got his lawyer into 'the most unpredictable problems.' Moosbrugger's nebulous defence strategy: he had murdered neither with intent nor was he insane; he had experienced no excitement and only reacted to this 'caricature of a woman' (74–5); as he explored the motivations of his actions, he could only find 'shadowy reasonings' and the format of a life that 'is always losing and changing shape' (76). While the tactic of the court consists in connecting events in a logical order and subjecting them to a judgement, for Moosbrugger the deed is composed of single, unrelated incidents that do not cohere as a complete case in the world of the court. The perpetrator has become his own fabulous cosmos.

This marks an important and systematic shift in forensic procedure. Moosbrugger's case is situated in a precarious 'neither–nor' or 'both–and' that characterizes fragile health as much as a minor illness—a limit case that produces, under the name of 'diminished responsibility', an ambiguous situation. Fragile health means fragile responsibility, which is still responsibility; it sets into motion the juridical machine of judgement and punishment. Minor illness, on the other hand, means irrationality and therefore mental incapacity and therefore the suspension of the juridical machine. What results is a blockage in the system: while Moosbrugger's sanity falls under the law, the analysis of his illness does not come to an end and must capitulate—as do 'the angel of medicine' (262) and psychiatry—before a decision. The halfway intelligent subject and the halfway incomprehensible deed lead to a reciprocal paralysis that imperils the legal proceedings and produces a kind of casuistry that reaches from Musil's novel deep into the nomological knowledge of the law. Already in the debates at the turn of the century, in the writings of Franz von Liszt, for example, the problematic notion of 'diminished responsibility' led to the question of whether the legal ability of rendering judgement has not reached its limit. In the novel, the same question is raised by Ulrich's father, a man of the court and a late follower of Liszt's social and sociological school, who sharpens it into an unexpected paradox. The healthy perpetrator is capable of being punished and does not create further problems. The sick perpetrator is not only incapable of responsibility but most often he is also more dangerous; the more dangerous a crime and a perpetrator are, the more they are worthy of punishment; which in turn leads to the drastic paradox:

> Hence the more dangerous he is, the more responsible he is for his actions, with the inescapable logical consequence that those criminals who seem to be the most innocent, the mentally sick, who are by nature least susceptible to correction by punishment, must be threatened with the harshest penalties, harsher than those for sane persons, so that

the deterrent factor of punishment be equal
for all (587).[13]

He who is unfit for punishment requires punishment
to the highest degree, and diminished responsibility
is really heightened responsibility. A system of distinctions and judgements leads to its own indiffer-
ences and paradoxes; the capital punishment for
Moosbrugger is only preliminary and does nothing to
relieve the fundamental perplexity. Thus is set the
methodological path of Musil's novel, its 'fantastic
exactitude'. First, it follows individual events into their
farthest nooks and crannies. From Moosbrugger's
deed we get to the circumstances, from the circumstances to the motive, from the motive to the side-
motives and from those to a complicated physiological, nervous and psychic apparatus. In the course of its
analysis, a simple deed loses its contours, liquefies and
leads into uncharted territory. It leads into an 'infinite
system of relationships' (270) in which independent
signification, simple deeds and attributes do not exist.
Furthermore, fantastic exactitude generates a specific
knowledge that paradoxically has to be called knowledge of the particular or science of the individual.
While the procedures of pedantry only know the repetition of the particular in the universal and, therefore,
resemble 'the attempt of the fool trying to spear a
free-flying bird with a bin' (267), the fantastic method
concentrates on the facts and with them can only state
that the case of Moosbrugger does not fit under a
general law nor corresponds to a known pathology.
A knowledge of specificity is thereby generated that
is in itself inconclusive and endless: 'the experts never

*Fall of the
System of
Judgement*

finish anything' (215). Two ways of questioning
are opposed here: on the one hand, deed or fact is
examined by the question: 'what is?'; by the question
of substance or essence which supposedly can be
answered by a general concept. On the other hand,
deeds and facts are surrounded by circumstantial
questions which could be called positivistic or crimi-
nological: not 'what is?', but 'how?', 'under what
circumstances?', 'in which case?', 'in what respect?',
'where?', 'why?', 'when?' ... Facts in this case appear less
as cases than as events that are unfolded into all their
parts and components, into their circumstances, probabilities and conditions. Fantastic exactitude probes
the folds of facts and gives rise to an art of making distinctions that, in turn, can be understood as criticism
only insofar as it provokes a crisis, an overthrow of systems of judgement. Where the pedantic procedure
sees a case, knows the law, and judges with good reasons, fantastic work transforms reasons into ground-
lessness and blocks every efficient judgement. From its
perspective, the world is everything that is not the
case; it reveals the principle of a missing reason. Events
and predicates do not converge in a concept. The
result is completely impractical and inconsequential,
better yet: it is adumbrated by the premonition that
'no thing, no self, no form, no principle' (269) can be
regarded as durable and safe. In the facticity of the
case an inner potential is thereby disclosed, justifying
Ulrich's repeated idea: 'if mankind as a whole could
dream, that dream would be Moosbrugger' (77).

Revision   With considerable energy, Musil thus has defined the
man without qualities as a man who tarries, as a man

of possibilities and, by consequence, as a man of dif-
ferences; his procedure—the fantastically exact operations—turns tarrying into a method. This exactitude
appears as the intellectual substrate of tarrying as a
function; it shows a 'paradoxical interplay between
exactitude and indifference' (246). Thus the space is
opened in which the discourse of the novel unfolds.
In the system of tarrying, analysis, differentiation and
multiplication of the factual lead to the place where
judgement as a form is deactivated and the measure of
man itself is suspended.

If this system propagates a radical 'critique of the
court of law', its address is a specifically modern conception of what constitutes order and orderliness. If it
is true that every modern form of order is selective and
exclusive, that it operates with preferences the origin
of which it cannot justify, then, as Nietzsche says,
there is 'an abyss behind every ground, under every
"groundwork" a chasm that can be bridged neither
cosmologically nor normatively'.[14] The principle of
insufficient reason and the procedure of fantastical
exactitude are complementary in this respect, as they
make visible the positivity of an order that is neither
random nor necessary: it is marked by residual forms
without claims to totality, by normative regulations
without an ultimate reference, by a network of facts
without governing rationality. The differential analysis of lead distinctions ends in a zone of haziness in
which, as in Moosbrugger's 'reduced responsibility',
the excluded third returns and insists as that which
cannot be differentiated. The procedure of tarrying
accomplishes a recursive motion and takes aim at the
horizon on which the continuous transformation of

disorder into order happens. The principle of insufficient reason serves in Musil's novel as a guiding thread and is motivated by a positivism of which it is not yet decided whether it is gay or gruesome. From this perspective, the ground of systems of order and judgement is nothing but their positive existence; the fantastically exact inquiry deciphers what is dissimilar in all equations, the arbitrary and the posited in all lawfulness. The suspicion harboured by tarrying and its exact method concerns the durability of initial and concluding reasons, and the legitimacy of a first—and a last—word. Its discourse is in a constant state of revision. Methodical tarrying produces a 'peculiar mirage' in which 'life-as-it-is strikes us as fragmented by life-as-it-might-be'. Tarrying and fantastic exactitude belong to the doctrine of method of a universal history of contingency; they urge us not to forget the search for the 'fulfillment of the promises sunk into the world' (1391).

Notes

1   Théobule Ribot, *The Diseases of the Will* (Chicago: Open Court Publishing Company, 1915), pp. 33–4, 43. (the author mentioned is Thomas de Quincey). A prime example of a socio-technical discourse on the connections of industrial society and fatigue is the writing of Angelo Mosso (*Fatigue*. New York: G. P. Putnam's Sons and London: S. Sonnenschein, 1904). See also Anson Rabinbach, *Human Motor: Energy, Fatigue, and the Origins of Modernity* (New York: Basic Books, 1990), *passim*.

2   Ribot, *The Diseases of the Will*, p. 46.

3   Oscar Berger, 'Die Grübelsucht: Ein psychopathisches
    Symptom' ('The Addiction to Ruminate: a Psycho-
    pathic Problem') in *Archiv für Psychiatrie und Nerven-
    krankheiten* 6 (1876): 226–8; Wilhelm Griesinger,
    'Ueber einen wenig bekannten psychopathischen Zus-
    tand' ('On a Little-Known Psychopathic State of Mind')
    in *Archiv für Psychiatrie und Nervenkrankheiten* 1,
    (1868–69): 629–32.

4   Ribot, *The Diseases of the Will*, pp. 20–4, 27

5   Robert Walser, *The Robber* (Susan Bernofsky trans.) (Lin-
    coln: University of Nebraska Press, 2000), p. 95. Wolf-
    gang Koeppen, *The Hothouse* (Michael Hofmann trans.)
    (New York and London: W. W. Norton, 2001), p. 210.

6   Paul Valéry, 'Monsieur Teste' in *Collected Works of Paul
    Valery*, VOL. 6 (Jackson Mathews trans.) (Princeton:
    Princeton University Press, 1956–75), pp. 3, 43.

    In their commentaries on Melville's Bartleby—the very
    model of capability and the abrogated act—Deleuze
    and Agamben have just about said it all. See Gilles
    Deleuze, 'Bartleby, or The Formula' in *Essays Critical
    and Clinical* (Daniel W. Smith and Michael A. Greco
    trans) (Minneapolis: University of Minnesota Press,
    1997), pp. 68–90. Giorgio Agamben, 'Bartleby, or On
    Contingency' in *Potentialities: Collected Essays on Phi-
    losophy* (Daniel Heller-Roazen trans.) (Stanford, Stan-
    ford University Press, 1999), pp. 243–71.

7   Robert Musil, *The Man Without Qualities* (Sophie
    Wilkins trans.) (New York: Alfred Knopf, 1995), p.
    276. (Further citations and their page numbers refer to
    this edition.)

8   Gottfried Wilhelm Leibniz, *Opuscules et fragments
    inédits* (Short Works and Unpublished Fragments)
    (Louis Couturat ed.) (Hildesheim: George Olms,
    1966), p. 533. Pierre-Simon Laplace, *Essai philo-
    sophique sur les probabilités* (Philosophical Essay on
    Probability) (Paris: Fayard, 1984,), p. 32. On this and

the following, see also Jacques Bouveresse, 'Nichts geschieht mit Grund: Das "Prinzip des unzureichenden Grunds"' ('"Nothing Happens for a Reason": the Principle of Insufficient Reason') in Mary-Louis Roth and Bernhard Böschenstein (eds), *Hommage à Musil* (A Homage to Musil) (Berne and New York: P. Lang, 1995), p. 111–41.

9   See Gilles Deleuze, *The Fold: Leibniz and the Baroque* (Tom Conley trans.) (Minneapolis and London: University of Minnesota Press, 1993), pp. 41–2.

10 Ibid., pp. 80–1.

11 Adolphe Quételet, *Soziale Physik oder Abhandlung über die Entwicklung der Fähigkeiten des Menschen* (Social Physics, or Treatise on the Development of Human Capabilities), VOL. 1 (Jena: G. Fischer, 1914), pp. 106–07.

12 See Agamben, 'Bartleby'.

13 On the discussion of criminal law, Franz von Liszt and the sociological school with reference to Musil, see Stefan Andriopoulos, *Unfall und Verbrechen: Konfigurationen zwischen juristischem und literarischem Diskurs um 1900. Hamburger Studien zur Kriminologie* (Accident and Crime: Configurations of Juridical and Literary Discourses around 1900. Hamburg Studies in Criminology), VOL. 21 (Pfaffenweiler: Centaurus, 1996), pp. 71–82, 115–30. On specific blockades in the mechanism of punishment, how they have brought with them the question of attribution and especially the intervention of psychiatry since the nineteenth century, see Michel Foucault, *Abnormal: Lectures at the Collège de France, 1974–1975* (Graham Burchell trans.) (New York: Picador, 2003), p. 113–9.

14 Friedrich Nietzsche, *Beyond Good and Evil: Prelude to a Philosophy of the Future* (Judith Norman trans.) (Cambridge: Cambridge University Press, 2002), p. 173.

CHAPTER FIVE

LABYRINTHS, THRESHOLDS

So far, we have detailed three perspectives through
which tarrying tends towards a systematic orientation
of its mode of questioning: first, through a problematic structure that persists in all of its answers and solutions; second, through the reference to a mode that
places all events in a frame of contingency; third,
through a method of inquiry that disorganizes the system of law and judgement. With these characteristics,
the discourse of the twentieth century has itself turned
into a drawn-out tarrying; it follows a digressive path
and gains its significance in a certain reserve against
that what is as it is. Against this background, we can
detect a splitting of the discursive field that determines
up to today the order of discourse and the possibility
of its analysis.

In the system of literature, we can recognize a
trope that infallibly turns to those nodes where a text
negotiates the diversity of its possible continuance and
becomes, as it were, infinite. The point is, as Valéry
remarked, to capture the form of a work at the moment
of its becoming-form, to chose a path that evokes for
every act, for every sentence, for every position an act,
sentence and position that is also possible and that

Knots

81

leads from bifurcations to bifurcations of bifurcations. To be able to hesitate, to hesitate in a prolonged and sustained manner, emerges as the absolute condition at the threshold of form. 'It would be interesting', Valéry wrote in 1937,

> to produce *at least once* a work that would exhibit at its nodal points the manifold that presents itself to the mind and from which it selects the only consequence that the text then pursues. This would mean that one should replace the illusion of a singular and mimetic definition of the real by an at-all-times-possible that seems to me much closer to the truth.[1]

Aesthetically, this amounts to an undoing of the work, systematically, to a re-entry of form into form; within the logic of movement, however, it generates a parcours of tarrying in which the form of the labyrinth is repeated in the labyrinth of form. The format of discourse itself has become labyrinthine; it measures itself against a labyrinth whose form follows the torn thread of Ariadne. Insofar as we can call, with Benjamin, the labyrinth 'the habitat of the dawdler',[2] it exhibits the pace of tarrying itself. One of the main problems of modern poetics consists in telling various divergent stories at the same time and in generating a system that refers to systems of systems;[3] and these are populated by figures who specialize in getting lost.

Disjunctive Synthesis

What could be called 'world' in such a constellation has no more than hypothetical existence. One example is the 'The Garden of Forking Paths', the model narrative from Borges' *Fictions* in which he lets everything happen at once: people can kill or be killed, kill and be killed at the same time, escape together or and at the same time die together: 'Fang, let us say, has a secret. A stranger knocks at his door. Fang makes up his mind to kill him. Naturally there are various possible outcomes. Fang can kill the intruder, the intruder can kill Fang, both can be saved, both can die and so on and so on.'[4] This literature finds its material in the gathering of incompossibilities and in a 'world of all possibilities'; it finds its formal procedure in a disjunctive synthesis, in a synthesis in which one and the other, 'both–and' is expressed, in which that which does not belong together is written together. Disjunctive syntheses structure an arrested in-between and make use of a potential for getting lost and confused that fills out the interval of tarrying.

Phenomenologically speaking, at least two different perspectives and modalities emerge. The first, external mode appears as a mere hesitation that is characterized by a peculiar emptiness in the mysterious gap between decision and execution: nothing happens. On the question, for example, of what happens when one wants to pick up an object from the ground and then really does so, the following conversation between Samuel Beckett and his biographer James Knowlson addressed the void of the intervening moment. Here is the record of this conversation from 1955:

> There often *is* a 'between'. 'I will get out of bed.' One doesn't. 'I will get out of bed.' And then one does, as if by magic. By magic being what we don't understand. I told him, one says to someone in a catatonic stupor apparently,

'Make an effort of will.' Ridiculous. 'Make an effort of will.' Still nothing. One talks, exhorts. Even shakes them. There is no response. When they begin talking lucidly as if their earlier rigidity had never happened, one can never know what made them break the circle, within which they circled. One moment they were in it, then not. Beckett said, 'It is as if there were a little animal inside one's head, for which one tried to find a voice; to which one tries to give a voice. That is the *real* thing. The rest is a game.'[5]

The other side of the catatonic paralysis and its mysterious void is the 'proper', a kind of standing stampede of discourse in which the animal in the head finds its own voice and language. It addresses the interval in a procedure of 'both–and' and loses itself in a litany of bifurcations, in the logic, or rather the schizo-logic of disjunctive syntheses. In Beckett's late story 'Enough', this is precisely articulated:

He sometimes halted without saying anything. Either he had finally nothing to say or while having something to say he finally decided not to say it [. . .] Other main examples suggest themselves to the mind. Immediate continuous communication with immediate redeparture. Same thing with delayed redeparture. Delayed continuous communication with immediate redeparture. Same thing with delayed redeparture. Immediate discontinuous communication with immediate redeparture. Same thing with delayed redeparture. Delayed discontinuous communication with immediate redeparture. Same thing with delayed redeparture.[6]

The immediate and the delayed, the discontinuous and the redeparted block one another; the syntax of the text hesitates and tarries because the semantics of its sentences branches out and accumulates and always ends, despite constant substitution and change, with the 'same' result. The disjunctive syntheses hold the text back as it proceeds, and transform it into that in-between: endless oscillation, and the foundation of modern literary logic.

But it was probably Kafka's procedure that elevated labyrinthine discourse and its sustained tarrying to its inner principle and its law of formation: full of beginnings and new beginnings, repetitions and bifurcations that never lead to unity, to an end or an exit. Repetition is quite apparently the medium of this literature. Just as Kafka in his diaries speaks of 'the misery of having perpetually to begin' and of the illusion 'to advance the ball',[7] so his literature presents itself as a series of attempts and inceptions that break off after the first sentence, sometimes make it to a second or third sentence, rarely reach the size of a novella or novel, and if so lead nowhere and rarely end with the consent of their author. Kafka's texts meander, do not or only with difficulty make it beyond their own beginning and lose themselves in preliminaries.

More precisely, however, Kafka's texts provide something akin to a doctrine of thresholds. *The Castle*, for example, begins with an arrival that is immediately interrupted and then remains at the threshold:

Kafka

> It was late evening when K. arrived. The village lay under deep snow. There was no sign of the Castle hill, fog and darkness surrounded it, not even the faintest gleam of light suggested the Castle. K. stood a long time on the wooden bridge that leads from the main road to the village, gazing upward into the seeming emptiness.'[8]

The arrival is not an arrival, is interrupted at the moment of ingress—into the text, into the village—on the threshold, on the bridge by an apparent emptiness on which one looks as on a blank page. The beginning stagnates, the text commences with a tarrying, hesitating step.

At the very beginning, then, the expanse of a threshold is measured, of a limit that expands and that cannot be stepped over, and it is this zone of an interrupted beginning that structures the continuation of the path, of the narration, of the text. The next stop, the pub 'The Bridge' or 'Bridgehouse' repeats this pattern. K. immediately falls asleep, is woken up, falls asleep again, is repeatedly disturbed in his sleep only to awake again the next day. As he again takes up his journey, he continues in the repeated beginnings the initial hesitation. This is the way to the so-called castle: K. takes the main route from the village to the castle but the route does not lead that way. K. approaches the mountain and the castle but does not get any nearer and, as he moves forward step by step, station by station, the village seems to have 'no end' and allows only for lateral movement that combines continuous approach and renewed deviation in a single rhythm of tarrying:

So he set off again, but it was a long way. The street he had taken, the main street in the village, did not lead to the Castle hill, it only went close by, then veered off as if on purpose, and though it didn't lead any farther from the Castle, it didn't get any closer either. K. kept expecting the street to turn at last toward the Castle and it was only in this expectation that he kept going; no doubt out of weariness he was reluctant to leave this street, what amazed him, too, was the length of this village, which wouldn't end, again and again those tiny little houses and the frost-covered windowpanes and the snow and not a living soul— finally he tore himself away from this clinging street, a narrow side street took him in, the snow here was even deeper, lifting his sinking feet was hard work, he broke out in perspiration, suddenly came to a stop and could go no farther (10).

The way is a detour, its direction deviated and its path endless; K.'s own hesitation is doubled by the tarrying structure of the way, and ends in a frozen movement.

Another observation. While K., reminded by the distant view of the castle and its tower of the steeple in his hometown that 'decisively, without hesitation, and straight' points upwards and obviously is associated with a 'higher goal' (8), and therefore functions with its unique direction as a reference and a metaphor, its counterpart on the castle lacks any such orientation: initially 'clearly delineated' and 'easily and freely pointing' upwards, then weathered and unclear in its contours, finally completely 'uncertain, irregular, brittle, as if drawn by an anxious or careless child' (8), a disoriented heap of lines. The castle is less a castle than a drawing, and as a drawing not a drawing of a castle; as the visible form disappears, so too its referential, metaphorical dimension withdraws.

In the Castle

Thus emerges a topographical insecurity that determines the entire symbolic structure of the novel. On the one hand, K. will never cross the border, never get from the village to the castle; he will always be diverted and left to stumble around the periphery. On the other hand, it was obvious from the very beginning that while in the village one was already in the castle and that he who stays in the village is 'effectively residing or spending the night in the Castle' (2). If the village belongs in some ways to the castle, the castle does not necessarily belong to the castle. What is being said about it leads to the conclusion that one is not in the castle when one is in it. Of course, one can cross the border into the castle and enter the chancellery of the castle, and one can do this simply and without problems; 'but are the offices really in the castle? And even if the Castle does have offices' are those the offices that 'one is permitted to enter?' Of course—the novel goes on—one can enter the offices, 'but those are only a portion of the total, then there are barriers, and behind them more offices'. It is not all prohibited 'to go farther', and one must not 'imagine these barriers as a fixed boundary'. Barriers exist also 'within the offices' which one may enter; there are barriers that one may 'cross', and they 'look no different' from those 'one has not yet crossed'. That is why 'one shouldn't assume from the outset that the offices behind those other barriers differ significantly' (174–5). And so on. Barriers lead to further barriers, crossed borders to new borders; and what one has crossed returns in the same way, without beginning or end. One never reaches the castle and is always already there. The castle is nothing else than the threshold to the castle.

This results in a strangely structured space that is marked by borders that are immediately cancelled; a jagged space that becomes smooth; a smooth space on which markers and inscriptions float as if on the open sea. Since there is no real border between the village and the castle, the castle is represented less as a delineated *topos* and more as an infinite series of barriers and borders. All borders are always already or never crossed, disappear in the crossing and lead to other borders that lose themselves in indifference. The borders that refer from the margins of the novel to the inner topography of the castle, do not order, separate or distinguish its space. They mark and unmark at the same time, and they organize the entire (symbolic) space of the novel as a kind of threshold-zone. The threshold thus is the functional element of doubly interrupted transition and transport. As a 'wooden bridge' that K. at the beginning of the novel does (not) cross, it provides the parameters for all further measurements of space. As a metaphor of transit or transport it is at the same time metaphor of metaphor, it takes up the translation in *metaphorein* and marks at the beginning of the text a transition into the symbolic order of the castle that, at the same time, it interrupts. It therefore not only leads to the ominous castle, to the symbolic centre of the novel, but also to its de-symbolization which constitutes its power of reference and annuls it at the same time.

A similar procedure—to mention this briefly — characterizes the topography of *The Trial*: endless suites of chancelleries in the court; the remarkable privileging of threshold and transitory spaces like stair-cases, corridors and hallways; the surprising porosity and changeability of all rooms and halls which comprise and reject, loosen and change all possible functions, as they are used, at will, as nurseries, bedrooms, chambers, kitchens, living rooms, as offices or consultation rooms, as a theatre or court room—rooms with multiple functions that are not determined or coded in a univocal manner. Above all, the courtroom is represented in a manipulated, distorted and ultimately dissolved metric that does not fit into any dimensional order: at one time, Josef K. has to go to a suburb to present himself for an interrogation at court; at another, he goes to a suburb in the exact opposite direction to meet the court painter Titorelli, opens a door and is back at the chambers of the court. This generates a remarkable topography: two diametrically opposed places are contiguous; one goes into one direction and arrives in another. This space has no extension, no spatial, dimensional consistency. The most important piece of furniture is, therefore, the door: it is an element that gives and withholds structure, that seals and opens rooms, that provides and interrupts connections, that divides what belongs together and conjoins what is disparate. As a relay and switch it marks the threshold, the *fort* and *da*, the on and off of the symbolic order—the corridors of Kafka's bureaucracies resound with the noise of opening and closing doors.[9]

Just as the castle is both in the distance and every-where, the court in *The Trial* can be found nowhere and just round the corner. The K.s in *The Castle* and *The Trial* move in a borderless space of borders; and the infinite space of thresholds and transitions that knows no distinct borders may very well characterize the dawn of a state of waiting that expands between the no-longer and the not-yet, that is, as Benjamin said, entirely fluid and undetermined: 'The threshold must be carefully distinguished from the boundary. A *Schwelle* "threshold" is a zone. Transformation, pas-sage, wave action are in the word *schwellen*, swell.'[10]

Arbitrary Space

More precisely, the threshold in Kafka is part of a space that is structured less topographically than topologically. Kafka's transitional threshold space con-tains the code for the production of what one could call *Atopos*: neither a specific space nor a non-space but an un-spaced space, a spatial situation that makes every determined place quake and slip. This space has no firm foundation or ground and does not recognize the inscriptions of order and orientation.

Furthermore, this is not a homogenous and man-ageable space of extension and intuition in which one can proceed, in which one can move from far to close, from one point to another. It is, rather, an un-extended and pre-extended space, organized by the *spatium*, the interval. Its structure could be captured by the concept 'arbitrary space'—a space that dramatizes the interrup-tion of spatial extension at every turn. Coordinates, orientation and metrics are disturbed, and present space is a state of incompleteness, an embryonic room that consists of in-betweens, of discontinuous places and points. It has neither border nor horizon, neither interior nor expanse, and its openings only include further inclusions. Its generic principle is the zero-vector: without transition, every place can refer to every other place. It is a space of disconnected singularities and of virtual relations. And as much as in it this or that event manifests itself, it is nevertheless a vessel of unborn concretions.[11]

Against this background, the labyrinthine qualities of this inhomogeneous, literally immense space—the home of those who tarry—can be addressed more specifically. We can distinguish at least three forms of labyrinths which in turn characterize three different epochs. First, there is the classical, Greek labyrinth, the labyrinth of the thread. It has one entrance, one exit and a centre to which one path leads; it is unicursal. One cannot really get lost in it as it is characterized by a structure that leads, along confusing paths, to a dark centre. The critical question is what may be found in that centre.

Second, there is the baroque and mannerist labyrinth that became a predilection at European courts. It is, properly speaking, a maze: it has a centre, various entrances and exits but also dead ends and side arms where decisions have to be made. In this labyrinth, one can indeed get lost and advance only by trial and error; a solution, a real overview is possible only from a higher position. That is why it became an allegory of our earthly trials which too can be resolved only by intervention from above.

And third, there is the labyrinth that is distinct from these two in that it interrupts the continuity of every path, be it straight, looped or knotted. This labyrinth has the character of a network or a rhizome and differs from its alternatives in various ways. It does not extend on a plane and is not built on a homogenous surface but is a system of shafts that sprawls in all dimensions at the same time. That is why any possible path can lead immediately to any other possible path. It has neither centre nor periphery and it offers no position from which it could be viewed as a whole. This labyrinth is infinite—an infinitely sprawling interior space that knows no exterior, that makes the distinction between interior and exterior irrelevant and obsolete. Its path leads all exits back to themselves and opens only onto itself. There are neither Minotaurs nor saving threads. Some of these aspects are articulated in Kafka's late fragment on the burrow of the mole: paths, knots and spaces with unclear laws of distribution.[12] While this labyrinthine structure seems to be closely related to Kafka's literary topology, it does not yet fully describe it, as we will see.

So far, we can register several effects of this type of labyrinth in Kafka's work. Just as there are no 'real' places and one can therefore never be out of place, all determinations are bracketed, provisional or haunted by their opposite. Has K. 'wandered into' in the village (2), did he just happen to arrive there, or has the Lord of the Castle 'sent for him'? (3) Is he there as a 'vagrant' or as a 'surveyor'? And can the 'surveying' of the land, which never actually happens, be understood as measurement or as mis-measurement or just

In Suspense

as measurelessness? The undecidability in this world is continued in its 'appearance' and accompanied by a form of questioning that works itself into all determinations. If borders are distinctions and distinctions are binary, then the logic of distinctions is suspended by the infinite recursiveness of its distinctions: K. is here and not here, in the village, in the castle, not here and here, not in the village, not in the castle . . . just as, at the beginning of the novel, 'not even the faintest gleam of light' shines on a 'seeming emptiness' (3), so too the power of appearances or of outright falsehood dominates in the textual labyrinth.

This uncertainty follows a precise methodology. In particular, the efficacy of Kafka's bureaucracy is afflicted by diminished responsibility and active suspension. He describes its mode of operation in laborious detail:

> And now I'm going to talk about a special feature of our official apparatus. In keeping with its precision it is extremely sensitive. When a matter has been deliberated on at great length, it can happen, even before the deliberations have ended, that suddenly, like lightening, in some unforeseeable place, which cannot be located later on, a directive is issued that usually justly, but nonetheless arbitrarily, brings the matter to a close. It's as if the official apparatus could no longer bear the tension and irritation stemming year in year out from the same perhaps inherently trivial affair and had all by itself, without help from the officials, made the decision. Of course, there was no miracle and some

official or other certainly wrote the directive
or reached an unwritten decision, at any rate
one cannot determine from down here, or
indeed even from the administrative offices,
which official reached the decision in this
case and on what grounds ... Now, as I said,
it's precisely these decisions that are mostly
excellent, the only disturbing thing is that
one only gets to hear about them when it's
too late, for one is still passionately dis-
cussing the matter that has long since been
resolved (68).

The bureaucratic apparatus works approximately
in approximation; it is congruent with the topology
that gathers disconnected places and that is organized
according to the torn thread, to the connecting mistake. It therefore severs any clear and predictable relation of reason and decision, of cause and effect, and
presents itself as an ensemble of more or less accidental
events. Decisions don't decide anything and miss the
cases in question, and what really happens forms a discontinuous trace that loses itself in the distance. The
institution remains in a peculiar in-actuality and follows the principle of a missing, insufficient reason.
Following the principle of ambiguity, it posits difference in identity and identity in difference, and thereby
generates the specific world-situation of *The Castle*.
The two apprentices coming from the castle, for example, remain indistinguishable, and therefore share one
first name; conversely, one single civil servant 'easily takes
on a variety of shapes in the imaginations of people'
(181) and may be confused with any other. If the principle of sufficient reason in a simple Leibnizianism

requires the reciprocal coordination of concept and thing, then it is precisely this coordination that is now blocked—by a proliferation of identical individuals, or by one individual who is interchangeable with all others. The result is a series of repetitions that remain conceptually undifferentiated and, therefore, cannot be represented, memorized or recognized. Similarities are misleading, distinctions produce confusion.[13]

In this way, literal blanks are produced. The accreditation, which K. neither receives nor not receives, has the character of an official proclamation whose reading results in a blank sheet that resists any hermeneutic effort: 'Chairman,' said K., 'you interpret the letter [of accreditation] so well that all that's finally left is a signature on a blank sheet of paper' (71). Like the 'judicial organ' in *The Trial*, the bureaucratic and worldly events in *The Castle* remain 'in a state of eternal equilibrium'.[14] The elementary activity of this bureaucracy, its procedure and specific method seem to consist in the crossing-out and cancellation of its own acts and files. The space of the castle presents itself as an infinite series of barriers and gates; it is this drawn-out threshold and barrier itself. It is, therefore, no wonder that the decisions, the ukase, communications and directives from this world are themselves barriers and barred: crossed-out.

Line as Labyrinth   The arrest and the threshold are thus the basic syntactic elements of Kafka's Castle that (de-)structure its text and his narrative, its space and its scripture; they raise fundamental questions of syntagmas and syntaxes, of joining and coordination. From here, a more precise analysis of the spatial and textual labyrinth and of its specific function of tarrying is possible. It is not only a matter of transforming the labyrinthine discourse from myth to mode of narration[15] but of the fundamental transformation of story and plot. First of all, Kafka's labyrinth is not a meandering or complicated way, not an erroneous way but no way at all. That is its historically new and systematic dimension. Kafka once said that there might be a destination but no way—'what we call a way is a tarrying'[16]—and thereby gave an elementary definition of his labyrinth. It is a sequence of intervals or blanks; more precisely, it results from infinitesimal divisions that separate ever-smaller sections into yet smaller ones. The labyrinth is an infinite process of interpolation, an arbitrary set of intervals within a continuum. That line is labyrinthine, is arrested at each of its points, changes directions, branches out and becomes non-linear. Since the nineteenth century, mathematicians have called such functions 'nowhere differentiable'; they unfold in a 'monstrous oscillation' and remain entirely non-intuitive. The way or the continuum is no longer, as Aristotle had postulated, that which cannot be divided and that which can be traversed from beginning to end; rather, the line is scanned point by point and leads to a kind of continuous occupation with every interval, however small.[17]

This abysmal and atomized continuum has a counterpart in a paradox that looks like an illustration of Kafka's labyrinth and that was first formulated by the mathematician Herrmann Hankel in 1870. A square with a side of 1 is divided by horizontal and vertical parallels into a lattice of small squares. The path from the lower left to the upper right corner—

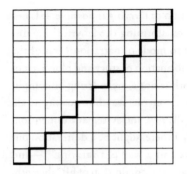

FIGURE 3. The curve as labyrinth: step curve according to Hermann Hankel.

whether one takes the base line and the right vertical, or any other path—is always = 2. If one chooses, however, a path that follows as close as possible along the diagonal in a series of steps, and if one increases the numbers of squares to infinity, the infinitely stepped curve coincides with the diagonal and results in a paradox: The path taken by the stepped curve is still = 2, but at the same time $\sqrt{2}$, the path of the diagonal. In reality, the limit curve of the diagonal is of a completely different nature: while the tangent of the diagonal has for all its points the same value or angle, the tangent of the stepped curve changes in each of its points from 0° to 90°. At none of its points does the limit curve have a definitive orientation. Not only is its length different from the diagonal, at each of its infinite number of points its continuation and orientation is in jeopardy (see Figure 3).[18] This results in the labyrinth of a line that 'errs' at each of its points, that branches out and interrupts the continuity of its path, that continuously tarries on its way. While Kafka's threshold space of *The Castle* does not correspond to the geometry of spatial extension, it obviously converges with the problems of modern analysis. Next to Kafka and modern

FIGURE 4. Paul Klee,
*Hauptweg und
Nebenweg* (Main
Path and Side
Path), 1929.

mathematics, perhaps only Klee has attempted to
graph this labyrinth of lines (see Figure 4).

Like the mathematics of the nineteenth century,
Kafka's literature, its doctrine of space and thresholds,
has discovered the labyrinth of the line, the line as
labyrinth; aside from the various aphoristic formula-
tions ('yes, the flying arrow is at rest'[19]), we can detect
here an original and material rewriting and notation
of the problem of tarrying and of the will—of the
question of how it manifests itself not as a conditioned
choice but as a choice that is undecided between
choosing and not-choosing. Kafka's labyrinthine line

Graph
of the Will

99

is the continuously tarried way. In a brief reflection, Kafka once articulated this connection:

> A man has free will, and this of three kinds: first of all, he was free when he wanted this life; now, of course he cannot go back on it, for he is no longer the person who wanted it then, except perhaps in so far as he carries out what he then wanted, in that he lives.
>
> Second, he is free in that he can choose the pace and the road of this life.
>
> Third, he is free in that, as the person who will sometime exist again, he has the will to make himself through life under every condition and in this way come to himself, and this, what is more, on a road that, though it is a matter of choice, is till so very labyrin-thine that there is no smallest area of this life that it leaves untouched.
>
> This is the trichotomy of free will, but since it is simultaneous it is also a unity, an integer, and fundamentally is so completely integral that it has no room for any will, free or unfree.[20]

The argument consists of two halves or parts that refer to one another without mediation. On one side, it provides the supposition of a radically free will, of a choice that has to be available at every moment of one's life: first, from the beginning and oriented towards the future; second, in retrospect, concerning the affirmation of lived life; and third, at every point of one's life that confronts one anew with the choice of choosing.

On the other side is the labyrinthine graph. If this 'electable' path 'leaves no speck of life' untouched, it results not only in an infinitely convoluted line but also in a line that changes direction in each of its segments, that fills out every 'speck', that is no longer a line but a scattering of points, each of which jeopardizes anew the orientation and the continuation of a life. The path, therefore, is not simply labyrinthine but 'labyrinthine to such a degree' that there is no longer a discernable direction: a monstrous oscillation. This, in turn, reproduces free will as a diagram: only when the graph of the will no longer indicates a single direction but comprises all 'at the same time' and thereby traces something similar to hachures in which all definitive directions are dissolved into indecidablity, only then does free will find its expression. But as such it does not appear as free will, or as its opposite, but as 'indifference': free will as the choice to choose becomes evident only if it does not actualize itself in this or that biography but in all possible lives—and therefore in none individually. Where there is a will there is not a way but all possible ways, and therefore a labyrinth. And in this respect, there is no way—only a 'tarrying'.

Only a few years later, Kafka's graph of the will was formulated on different kinds of paper but with a comparable result: as *Entscheidungsproblem*, decision problem. Refuting David Hilbert's claim that a universal method of distinguishing between decidable and undecidable problems is possible in mathematics, Alan Turing in 1937 implicated his universal machine in infinite tarrying. In layman's terms, the problem can briefly be described thus. There are two machines: one works non-circuitously, that is, it computes a calculable sequence and comes to rest after a finite set of operations. The other machine works circuitously: it computes incalculable sequences and thus enters into a state without exit or end. With these machines, decidable problems can be distinguished from undecidable ones. The next step is to conceive a machine that can distinguish from the set of all machines the circuitous ones from the non-circuitous ones and that, therefore, can make a distinction between decidability and undecidability. To this end, a machine H, which itself is non-circuitous and passes through finite calculations, is fed a set of machines: it marks the non-circuitous ones from the circuitous ones, that is, every time it encounters a circuitous machine, it excludes it (N − 1) and proceeds to examine the next machine (N + 1). It can produce a list of possible machines and exclude the impossible ones on a list N − 1. In order to decide the decision problem in the case of all machines, however, machine H has to simulate itself, that is, it has to introduce its own process of deciding into the set of computable operations. When it receives the command to examine its own operations—at the moment when its own number, its own algorithm appears in the set of machines to be examined—it performs the entire examination once again: examines and sorts the set of machines, excludes the impossible ones, then encounters its own algorithm again, begins the operation anew, computes the sequence again—an infinite encapsulation, an infinite recursion. The machine has a halting problem. But since machine H is defined as a non-circuitous machine, its mode of operation stands in contradiction with its decision; it is circuitous and non-circuitous at the same time, decides and does not decide: it cannot possibly exist. The problem of a decision between decidability and undecidability cannot be decided—faced with this decision problem, the machine begins to tarry and falls into its own kind of 'brooding dependence.' The problem can at best be delegated to a higher-order machine and faces an endless regress.[21] With its endless procedure, Turing's impossible machine digs through the sufficient reason of all mathematical proofs, without results. Like Kafka's labyrinthine graph, the computational path of this —impossible— machine always returns onto itself.

If Kafka's literature (and Turing's argument) can be understood as the attempt to refer the metaphysics of the will and of decision to its mysterious unfounding by means of the labyrinth, then the problem of continuation and of tarrying will by necessity influence the material process of writing. Indeed, we can observe that Kafka's writing of *The Castle* in the first months of 1922 begins to stumble whenever the paper of one of the quarto notebooks is used up and the 'jump into the open, into the uncertainty of an empty notebook'[22] is imminent. The syntax of the notebook is interrupted, disturbances increase, disorder expands: obviously, the arrival of a new material basis of writing necessitates decisions as to how the text, the writing, the narrative can be continued at all.

A particularly telling example is the end of the third and the beginning of the fourth Castle notebook; the subject of the text and the narration is a long conversation between K. and Olga about the messenger Barnabas' experiences and the chancelleries and

Writing and Tarrying

barriers of the castle's administration. The third notebook ends with a reflection on the interchangeability
of the administrators, on the lack of 'reference points'
in the bureaucratic machine, on the 'insecurity' of all
positions and decisions and on the precarious situation of all involved. Olga's last sentences in Kafka's
notebook are:

> How suspicious and threatening everything
> must seem to him there if he doesn't even
> dare to open his mouth and ask an innocent
> question. Whenever I reflect on this I accuse
> myself of leaving him [Barnabas] alone in
> those unknown rooms where the things that
> go on are such that even he, who is timid
> rather than cowardly, surely trembles with
> fear (182).

With this, the last page of the notebook is filled,
the text is interrupted and the continuation in the next
notebook, once it is conceived, cannot conceal a
certain gesture of decisiveness: 'Here, I think, you're
coming to the decisive point, said K. That's it. After
hearing all you've said, I think that now I can see
clearly' (182).

But just this decisive continuation and this clar-
ity—which soon enough will get lost in the text—has
disappeared at the beginning of the fourth Castle
notebook. Here there is only a writing that initiates
nothing; deep inside the notebook are pages full of
corrections, erasures, new beginnings and variants of
new beginnings in which the writing searches for orientation and the problem of continuation articulates
itself. The first attempt to continue in the new note-

book begins like this: 'Don't you think that it is like this?' 'I have the impression,' said K. 'that you're perfectly open to me, and therefore I want to be open to you as well.' The second attempt: 'Don't you think that it is like this?' 'I don't know,' said K. And then a third: 'I don't understand you now, Olga,' said K.' The fourth finally takes a decisive turn: 'Here, I believe, you have reached what is decisive'—the beginning of a long passage that, however, is crossed out once more.[23] The bridge from one notebook to the other and the threshold to a new beginning are thus marked by questions, by not-knowing, not-understanding and repetitions; hesitation and tarrying manifest themselves in a multiplication of textual paradigms that supplement one another, cross one another out and miss syntagmatic connections. This suggests the following conclusion: it is as if Kafka had taken the measure of the threshold-space of the castle and the suspended representation of its world in the very process of writing. He breaks off and becomes disoriented at the site where the threshold emerges as a manifest barrier, where the (writing) surface ends, branches out and demands a distinction and a decision. Writing itself apparently has measured the inner infinity of the threshold and tarries in front of its transgression.

Another example shows a similar complication. It is a text that was written earlier than the passage from *The Castle* on a loose sheet of paper, cut out of one of the quarto notebooks. Here, too, the writing of the novel came to a halt and on the next sheet the narrative 'First Sorrow' took shape: the story of a trapeze artist who never leaves his elevated, swaying and suspended place high up 'in the vaulted domes of the

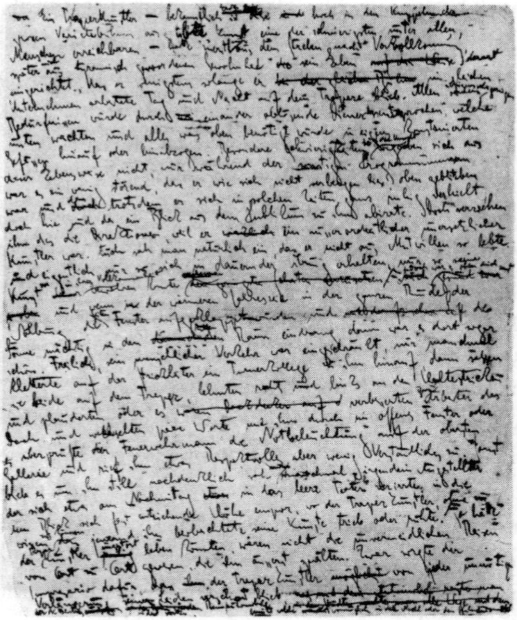

FIGURE 5. Franz Kafka, Facsimile of the short story 'Erstes Leid' ('First Sorrow') (front page).

great variety theatres' and whose only sorrow is the dramatic moment when he has to leave the trapeze and change location:

> The trapeze artist could have gone on living peacefully like that, had it not been for the inevitable journeys from place to place, which he found extremely trying. Of course his manager saw to it that his sufferings were not prolonged one moment more than necessary; for town travel, racing automobiles were used, which whirled him, by night if possible or in the earliest hours of the

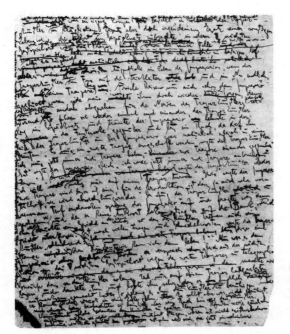

FIGURE 6. Franz Kafka, Facsimile of the short story 'Erstes Leid' ('First Sorrow') (reverse page).

morning, through the empty streets at breakneck speed, too slow all the same for the trapeze artist's impatience; . . . yet the manager never knew a happy moment until the trapeze artist set his foot on the rope ladder and in a twinkling, at long last, hung aloft in his trapeze.[24]

The problematic moment arrives when the state of suspension ends, when the ground is touched and the change 'from place to place' is imminent; the syntagmatic interruption in the text coincides with the change of sheets of paper. After the colon as a sign of caesura

('...was spared:'), the lines crowd the lower edge of the sheet, the handwriting becomes even smaller, and this text, too, begins to err at the transition from one place to another, from one sheet to another; it attempts various continuations, accumulates corrections and even changes into shorthand ('too slowly')—as if the pace of handwriting were too slow for the 'desire' of the writer, as if the interruption, the cut, the abyss in the trace of writing also needed to be bridged 'with utmost speed' or effort. Only when the continuation is found with the climb onto the new trapeze does the turbulence of erasures and variants subside. As if in a parallel commentary of the writing on itself, the trapeze as precarious and swaying perch of the artist corresponds to the empty page that can be left only at the price of interrupting the composition.[25]

Deactualization The syntax of the text and the process of writing, the narration and its graphic instantiation are obviously intertwined and point to a peculiar chiasmatic nature of this textual and writing situation. Where the text and the narration generate a suspension of representation, follow their inner infinity, accumulate indeterminations and succumb to a rhythm of tarrying, the writing keeps its decisive orientation and remains in continuous motion. Where the narration abandons its suspension, touches firm ground, transgresses a limit and takes a decisive turn—'from place to place', for example—the writing tarries and halts, and loses itself in various possibilities. Conversely: where the writing— at the end of a page or a notebook, for example—tarries, the narrative continues with renewed decisiveness. The result is a specific counter-punctual movement: the flow of writing apparently keeps the representation in suspension while its halting and hesitation makes appeals to ground and foundation, to distinction and decisiveness in the space of representation. The suspension of representation and the manifest process of writing, the hesitation in the handwriting and the decisive word enter into a relation of mutual dependence.

Thus might be described the systematic and historical place of this writing. With its specific version, Kafka's literature turns against an onto-theology of writing that perceives in writing an analogy to the act of creation, an emanation or manifestation of the spirit, a transition from a potential to its realization.[26] In Kafka's writing, no possible world is realized; on the contrary, his writing halts in front of bifurcations into different paradigms, in front of metaphorical alternatives and explicative passages and gains its footing above all in the generation of hermeneutic ambivalences.[27] As the trace or graph of tarrying, Kafka's writing keeps that difference or *différance* between potentiality and act that can neither be reduced to sheer potentiality nor to sheer actuality; it pursues in its writing the deferral of what is being written. The writing accomplishes a constant decision for the undecidable, its decisiveness concerns the act of deactualization; its play measures an incomplete world. In this respect, the labyrinth is a tarrying and the path of writing itself. Labyrinth and textual labyrinth are entwined. Kafka's writing process traces a path that measures only its inner infinity, that closes every exit back onto itself, that opens up only onto itself. That is Kafka's process: a progressive de-creation and a constant tarrying of the world's becoming.

If Kafka's writing can be conceived as a process of tarrying, as a continuous erasure of any first or last word,
this implies in its utmost consequence a blockage or
inhibition of eschatological movements. Eschatological energy passes by those who tarry, for God's invita-
tion to contribute to salvation does not suffer delay.
The psalmist says: 'I make haste and tarry not / to
keep your commands' (Ps. 119, 60). It is, therefore, not
surprising that Kafka tried his method of tarrying in a
corruptive reading of key passages in the Bible. The
most prominent example is probably Abraham, who
did not hesitate to obey God's word, call or charge
immediately, who got up early in the morning, left
his home, looked for the preordained place and began
the preparation for the slaughter of his son. In his
engagement with Kierkegaard's *Fear and Trembling*
and the decisive 'jump' of heroic faith, Kafka added a
few significant contortions and produced an Abraham
who presents himself as the most faithful hindrance
to God's plan. One could imagine, Kafka writes in 1921
to Robert Klopstock, 'another Abraham' who does
not become the patriarch, who does not even become
a 'dealer of old-clothes'. He is perfectly willing to exe-
cute the command immediately and subserviently 'like
a waiter' but then runs into difficulties and makes no
progress: 'because he cannot get away from home, he
is indispensible, the farm needs him, there is always
something that must be attended to, the house isn't
finished. But until the house is finished, until he has
this security behind him, he cannot get away. The
bible perceives this too, for it says: "He put his house
in order."' His house is not in order, and needs to be
looked after infinitely, and the incomplete business of

Abraham's world prevents the determinate Abraham from coming into existence. In addition, Kafka's non-biblical Abraham does not necessarily lack faith as such but faith in the possibility that he was meant as Abraham. Perhaps it's all just a result of mishearing things. He can understand himself only as a question that responds to the divine word, and therefore fears that 'he will ride out as Abraham with his son, but on the way will turn into Don Quixote' and end in ridicule.[28] Listening intently to the divine word, this Abraham never gets beyond tarrying.

Finally, in Kafka, the figure of Moses returns, this time strangely contorted and disfigured. The context is *The Trial*, its place of deployment the court of law; its problem, once again, consists in not being the judging, law-giving, sentencing, biblical Moses. Since the process in *The Trial* can never end, one never encounters real judges, or rather, one encounters them in images that are produced serially, that do not resemble any living exemplar and are nothing but pure fiction. What one encounters are variants of Freud's 'Moses of Michelangelo'. That, at least, is the way Kafka describes the serial portrait. On a 'throne' sits a 'man in a judge's robes', with 'a black bushy beard that hung far down the sides of his cheeks'; he does not sit 'in calm dignity', pushes 'his left arm braced against the back and arm of the chair', has 'his right arm completely free' and holds the armrest only with his hands 'as if he were about to spring up any moment in a violent and perhaps wrathful outburst to say something decisive or even pass judgment'. In addition, the portrait is done in 'pastel colors' which is 'not suitable' for 'such representations': because pastel, as a diminutive of 'pasta' (dough or paste), blurs the visibility of lines, contour and distinction, of a decisive form of judgement.[29] As a pastiche of judge and Moses, as image on a wall, the painting has only one possible place: as judge it blurs and blocks the form of judgement, as Moses it disfigures—as it did in Freud—the eschatological process.

In sum, Kafka's literature has dedicated itself to a procedure of tarrying whose productivity consists in the continuation of a textual labyrinth and in the sustaining of thresholds. One is related to the other. It cannot be overlooked that precisely this intermediate world has brought forth some of Kafka's most memorable characters: the incomplete and partially born, the hybrids, the infantile and indistinguishable assistants, eternally errant creatures or creatures that, alive and lifeless at the same time, defy any determination—like the hunter Gracchus who drifts on the 'infinitely wide and spacious stairs' between here and the beyond, or like Odradek with 'no fixed abode' in the stairway.[30] Kafka feels the deepest solidarity with these vagrant beings. Their existence is indeterminate, their realm is an in-between, a limbo at best—a place that is neither earthly nor heavenly nor hellish. That, at least, is how St Thomas Aquinas defined limbo: as a holding place for unbaptized children who have died without God, who will remain without God and who precisely for that reason do not lack anything. They are not blessed, because they are distant form the source of salvation; but perhaps they are a step closer to happiness, because they are unknowing and excepted from the distinction between the spheres of salvation and damnation. They remain, for the time being, tied to the 'in-between' and the zone of liminality: on the limits lie, as Lichtenberg once remarked, 'always the most curious creatures'.[31]

Notes

1   Paul Valéry, *Œuvres*, VOL. 1 (Jean Hytier ed.) (Paris: Gallimard, 1957), p. 1467. On this, see Stefan Lorenzer, 'Die Reflexion der Form: Eine Anmerkung zu Paul Valéry und Edmund Husserl' ('The Reflection of Form: A Note on Paul Valéry and Edmund Husserl') in Jürgen Schmidt-Radefeldt (ed.), *Paul Valéry: Philosophie der Politik, Wissenschaft und Kultur* (Paul Valéry: Philosophy of Politics, Science and Culture) (Tübingen: Stauffenburg Verlag, 1999), pp. 231–56. (Thanks to Karin Krauthausen for this reference.)

2   Walter Benjamin, 'Central Park' in *Walter Benjamin: Selected Writings, Volume 4: 1938–1940* (Howard Eiland and Michael W. Jennings eds) (Harvard: Harvard University Press, 2003), p. 171.

3   Italo Calvino, *Six Memos for the Next Millennium* (Patrick Creagh trans.) (Cambridge, MA: Harvard University Press, 1988), pp. 105–06.

4   Jorge Luis Borges, 'The Garden of Forking Paths' in *Fitcions* (Anthony Bonner trans., Anthony Kerrigan ed.) (New York: Grove Press, 1962), p. 98.

5   James and Elizabeth Knowlson, *Beckett Remembering, Remembering Beckett: Uncollected Interview with Samuel Beckett and Memories of Those Who Knew Him* (London: Bloomsbury, 2006), p. 111.

6   Samuel Beckett, 'Enough' in *Samuel Beckett: The Complete Short Prose 1929–1989* (S. E. Gontaskri ed.) (New York: Grove Press, 1995), p. 189. See Gilles Deleuze and Felix Guattarri, *Anti-Oedipus: Capitalism and Schizophrenia* (Robert Hurley, Mark Seem and Helen

R. Lane trans) (Minneapolis: University of Minnesota Press, 1983), pp. 13–14 (Beckett's story is cited here as an example).

7   Franz Kafka, *The Diaries of Franz Kafka, 1914–1923* (Martin Greenberg trans.) (New York: Schocken, 1949), p. 193

8   Franz Kafka, *The Castle* (Mark Harman trans.) (New York: Schocken, 1998), p. 1. (Further citations and page numbers refer to this edition.)

9   Gerhard Meisel, 'Türen: Zu Texten von Franz Kafka' ('Doors: on Texts by Franz Kafka') in Manfred Voigts (ed.), *Franz Kafka: 'Vor dem Gesetz:' Aufsätze und Materialien* (Franz Kafka: 'Before the Law': Essays and Materials) (Würzbug: Königshausen und Neumann, 1994), pp. 45–7. On spatial disorientation and threshold spaces in Kafka, see Stefan Gradmann, *Topographie/Text: Zur Funktion räumlicher Modellbildung in den Werken von Adalbert Stifter und Franz Kafka* (Topography/Text: On the Function of Spatial Models in the Works of Adalbert Stifter and Franz Kafka) (Frankfurt: Anton Hain, 1990), p. 135; Tobias Jentsch, *Da/zwischen: Eine Typologie radikaler Fremdheit* (In/Between: A Typology of Radical Strangeness) (Heidelberg: Universitätsverlag Winter, 2006), pp. 50–6.

10 Walter Benjamin, *The Arcades Project* (Cambridge, Belknap Press, 1999), p. 494.

11 See Deleuze, *Cinema 1*, pp. 108–11. On the paradigm of the threshold or bridge in Kafka, see Maurice Blanchot, 'Le pont de bois' ('The Wooden Bridge') in *De Kafka à Kafka* (From Kafka to Kafka) (Paris: Gallimard, 1981), pp. 185–201.

12 Franz Kafka, 'The Burrow' in *Complete Stories* (various trans., Nahum Glazer ed.) (New York: Schocken, 1971), pp. 325–59. On different types of labyrinths and their history, see Umberto Eco, 'The Detective Metaphysic' in his postscript to *The Name of the Rose* (William

Weaver trans.) (New York: Harcourt Brace, 1984), pp. 525–6. See also Hermann Kern, *Through the Labyrinth: Designs and Meanings over 5,000 Years* (Abigail H. Clay trans., with Sandra Burns Thomson and Kathrin A. Velder; Robert Ferré and Jeff Saward eds) (New York, Prestel, 2000).

13 Deleuze, *Difference and Repetition*, pp. 6ff.

14 Franz Kafka, *The Trial* (Breon Mitchell trans.) (New York: Schocken: 1998), pp. 119–20.

15 Manfred Schmeling, *Der labyrinthische Diskurs vom Mythos zum Erzählmodell* (The Labyrinthian Discourse from Myth to Narrative Model) (Frankfurt: Athenäum, 1987). Peter Utz, 'Das Labyrinth ist die Heimat des Zögernden: Robert Walsers "Minotaurus" und der labyrinthische Diskurs seiner Zeit' ('The Labyrinth is the Home of Those who Tarry: Robert Walser's "Minotaur" and the Labyrinthian Discourse of his Time') in *Runa* 21(1) (1994): 113–30.

16 Franz Kafka, *Blue Octavo Notebooks* (Ernst Kaiser and Eithne Wilkins trans, Max Brod ed.) (Cambridge: Exact Change, 1991), p. 23.

17 On the history of these 'monster' functions in analytical geometry, see Bernhard Siegert, *Passage des Digitalen: Zeichenpraktiken des neuzeitlichen Wissenschaften 1500–1900* (Passages of the Digital: Semiotic Practices of Modern Sciences 1500–1900) (Berlin: Brinkmann und Bose Verlag, 2003), pp. 313–23.

18 Ibid., pp. 323–5.

19 Kafka, *Diaries*, p. 34.

20 Kafka, *Blue Octavo Notebooks*, p. 50.

21 Alan Turing, 'On Computational Numbers, with Application to the Entscheidungsproblem' in *The Essential Turing* (B. Jack. Copeland ed.) (Oxford: Clarendon Press, 2004). (I would like to thank Bernhard Siegert for this reference and the patient explanation.)

22 Malcolm Pasley, 'Der Schreibakt und das Geschriebene: Zur Frage der Entstehung von Kafkas Texten' ('The Act of Writing and the Written: On the Question of the Origin of Kafka's Texts') in *Die Schrift ist unveränder-lich': Essays zu Kafka* ('Writing is Unchangeable': Essays on Kafka) (Frankfurt: Fischer Taschenbuch Verlag, 1995), p. 103. On stalling and straying in Kafka's 'methods', see Malte Kleinwort, *Kafkas Verfahren: Literatur, Individuum und Gesellschaft im Umkreis von Kafkas Briefen an Milena* (Kafka's Procedures: Literature, Individual and Society in the Context of Kafka's Letters to Milena) (Würzburg: Königshausen und Neumann, 2004), pp. 16, 36, 45–50. (Thanks to Malte Kleinwort for numerous suggestions.)

23 Franz Kafka, *Das Schloß, Apparatband*, pp. 351–67. See also pp. 42–5.

24 Franz Kafka, 'First Sorrow' in *Complete Stories*, p. 447

25 Franz Kafka, *Drucke zu Lebzeiten, Apparatband*, p. 407, pp. 412–3. See Wolf Kittler and Gerhard Neumann, 'Kafkas "Drucke zu Lebzeiten": Editorische Technik und hermeneutische Entscheidung' ('Kafka's "Publications during his Lifetime": Editorial Techniques and Hermeneutic Decisions') in Wolf Kittler and Gerhard Neumann (eds), *Franz Kafka: Schriftverkehr* (Franz Kafka: Scriptural Traffic) (Freiburg: Rombach, 1990), pp. 56–7. (Additional thanks to Gerhard Neumann for this reference.)

26 Agamben, 'Bartleby'.

27 Kittler and Neumann, 'Kafkas Drucke zu Lebzeiten', p. 45.

28 Franz Kafka, *Letters to Friends, Family, and Editors* (Richard and Clara Winston trans, Max Brod ed.) (New York: Schocken, 1977), p. 285.

29 Kafka, *The Trial*, pp. 105, 145. Pasley has noted the reference to Freud's 'The Moses of Michelangelo' and Kafka's possible reading on the subject: 'Two Literary

Sources of Kafka's *Der Prozess'*, *Forum for Modern Language Studies* 3 (1967): 142–7. Painted on the judge's throne is an allegory of justice, resembling more a 'goddess of victory' or 'goddess of the hunt'. The allegory presents a contamination of two figures related entirely to Freud's sense of the image of Moses in movement: one storming forward and another restraining itself. In the first draft Kafka depicted both figures separately and then merged them into a single figure (see Kafka, *Der Proceß, Apparatband*, p. 259).

30 Kafka, 'The Hunter Gracchus' in *Complete Stories*, p. 228, and 'The Cares of a Family Man' in ibid., p. 428.

31 Georg Christoph Lichtenberg, *The Waste Books* (R. J. Hollingdale trans.) (New York: New York Review Books, 1990), p. 48. On limbo in St Thomas Aquinas, see Giorgio Agamben, *The Coming Community* (Michael Hardt trans.) (Minneapolis: University of Minnesota Press, 1993), pp. 5–6.

CHAPTER SIX

IDIOSYNCRACIES

Passive/Active Tarrying and its textual equivalents are marked by an ambivalent figure. It is, first of all, implied in an artistry of errancy that performs a constant movement of evasion, that avoids the direct path, that takes up domicile in the labyrinth like in a world of bracketed determinations, in a region of diminished logic and consequence. The athletes of tarrying are all agents with a diminished share in the world, heroes with broken relations and therefore no heroes at all. They are motivated by the rupture in the sensorimotor connection, by the loosening of sensorimotor schemata that demotivate the transition from perception or reflection to action. What happens to them seems to concern them only partially; they manage to subtract from incidents and actions those parts that do not add up to the structure of events, that remain unfinished, deferred, unaccomplished or simply unrealized: 'I felt as if the incident had happened many years before or as if it hadn't happened to me or as if I had only heard people speak of it or as if I myself had forgotten it.'[1]

The unmistakable, individual and undividable part of an event is doubled by an impassivity that presents itself as impersonal and that characterizes a world full of fakery. The present, the time of acting and suffering, opens on a present-less time to which 'I' has no relation, in which 'I' has died or has remained unborn and experiences itself as the witness to an impossible experience. Here, the impersonal in every event is opposed to the event of the 'I'; here, to every moment corresponds 'something extra-temporal'; and here, the 'decisive moment' is always still and always imminent and keeps the action in suspense: 'The decisive moment in human evolution is perpetual [. . .] nothing has yet happened.'[2]

In this respect there is a loose connection between tarrying and an older catalogue of vices. Tarrying exhibits a distant relationship to the cardinal sin of sloth, *acaedia*. In its scholastic interpretation, sloth is not only the misdemeanour of inaction, the sickness that befalls monks who succumb to laziness and inactivity in the secluded spaces of contemplative life. Rather, it conjoins a diffuse unrest of the spirit with the pursuit of diverse and contingent objects without goal, without consistency, without serious purpose; a feverish relaxation. As the literary vice as such, *acaedia* looses itself in inane fictions, lets happen what happens anyway, fails to act and finally results in a kind of Hamletization of life and the world in an inaction with perhaps disastrous consequences. Above all, in its modern instantiation, it is characterized by a preference for evasion and avoidance, for intersections, for labyrinths and for non-linear time: it claims that there is never not enough time, that time is an inexhaustible and infinite source. Its darkest side, finally, is inert disbelief, nurtured by the discomfort entailed in the battles of faith. At the centre of *acaedia* is a stubborn sorrow in the face of God's Providence; the slothful has disregard for the meaningful end of history, and has cancelled his participation in the history of salvation. Not by accident did Dante place the slothful in a dromological order, on a kind of hellish and eternal jogging track.[3]

This, however, reveals a different perspective on tarrying: it reveals the active side of tarrying, distant from all substrates of inertia. This other side encompasses an idiosyncratic punctiliousness, an idiosyncrasy against the solidity of worldviews, against the irrevocability of judgements, against the finality of solutions, against the determinateness of consequences, against the duration of laws and the weight of results, as well as resolute diffidence against eschatological flights of fancy. Tarrying requests an appeal. It articulates a sense of complication that is less concerned with solutions to problems than with the supposition that in all given answers and solutions persist unresolved questions and problems. Surrounded by solutions, we do not necessarily find the problems that correspond to them. Tarrying harbours the suspicion of complexity and follows an arithmetic that multiplies questions exponentially. It cannot or will not bear the linearity and uniformity of the world: 'Now the fact is that the world is notoriously and uncommonly manifold, which can be put to the test at any moment if one just takes up a handful of World and looks at it a little more closely.'[4]

Repartee That is why tarrying has found its shadowy historical place where the hegemony of consequences, the finality of chains of actions and the inevitability of events and incidents is strongest. The trace element of tarrying in the action of tragic heroes is a case in point: it marks the drifting moment when action is wrested from the decisiveness of the gods, from the violence of their interventions and the power of fate, and consigned to a realm of terrestrial competence. The same systematic function of tarrying is also visible in modern contexts that have built their efficiency and dynamic stability on the basis of reliable automatisms: on the minimization of sovereign power and the predictability of individual intentions. The will to systematicity—or rather, the performance of the will in modern functional systems—directs choice, guides selection and renders the meaning of individual decisions contingent, if likely. If (social) systems operate under the condition of a constitutive weakness of knowledge and decision, tarrying condenses the collective consciousness in the system but positions itself as the antipode of the former sovereign. It may be that he who decides the state of exception is sovereign, but tarrying, the arrest between decision and non-decision, holds fast to the memory of evolutions and complex systems as themselves highly unlikely: What would it be like to return the sequences and consequences of actions, to this singular moment and unravel them?

Tarrying is particularly incisive within the horizon of our present, which is more and more characterized by the politics of preparedness for attack. Aiming and targeting make up its programme. Information is defined simply as an answer, and as the reduction and elimination of the distance between question and answer; all talk is formulated as response, precise and blow-by-blow. Above all, a new politics of 'targets of opportunity' has been put in place: it does not miss an opportunity to act, to strike first, to strike pre-emptively. To have power means to be able to mobilize in spite of persistent confusion, to deploy and to strike at any time. 'Opportunity' is a gate or a portal that has just opened; whatever the goal or the purpose (*telos*) of an initiated action may be, the decisive strike is directed at the target (*skopos*) visible in the opening. There are obvious signs that political fortune today, at the latest since the so-called war on terror, is defined by a highly excitable 'scopic activity' that is bound to its target opportunities: opportunities to overthrow the Taliban, to impose a new order on the Middle East, to destroy Saddam Hussein, to finish off this or that enemy.[5] The process of sounding out, addressing and identifying the enemy characterizes the state of exception and the infrastructure of a politics of the world as a homeland, of a new militarism that manages the fixed and moving, hard and soft, dubious or unknown targets that all of us are. Contemporary conceptions of the political must contend with the rationality of targeting and with the inevitability of its chain reactions. Sounding out and identifying an enemy happens under the imperative of a short and fleeting time in which any alternative assumption, and finally the appearance of the friend, would demand infinite hesitation. Without a doubt, politics is now constituted by the necessity to decide quickly, with all the preventative measures and post-operative consequences that implies.[6] Its defining moment, however, is no longer the sovereign decision but a helpless phrase that an absent God left behind at the end of Karl Kraus' *The Last Days of Humankind*: 'I did not want this.'

Against this background, tarrying innervates a specific sense of danger, a search into the role played by imagined or manifest dangers in the history of Western civilization. Tarrying carries the secret hope of a secular catechontic power. On the one hand, the ideas, visions and fantasies of what threatens us contain information on the ways in which the cohesion and the interfaces of a social and cultural order have been conceived. Just as the fury of Achilles not only gave rise to the first Western epic, but also to a lasting image of the ruin of the ancient world, so too all other reports about open or concealed dangers, about internal or external enemies, about catastrophic scenarios furnish perspectives on how societies renew and secure themselves by continuously banishing terror beyond the horizon. On the other hand, the manifest forms of danger, threat and risk constitute a dark and powerful reservoir of actions. What is addressed as a threat generates a logic that defines the possibility of response and encodes the field of action. Modern societies are drenched in a culture of danger; the collapse of any historical sense of possibility—of what Musil called *Möglichkeitssinn*—corresponds to today's speculative boom in security threats. That is why this discourse is so effective and at the same time so worthy of examination: the image of the great threat eliminates choice, denounces tarrying and leaves nothing but literally fatal perspectives.

Tarrying and its procedures characterize not only those who are allergic to action and full of hope for something better. The structure of the problematic, a 'fantastic' precision, the appeal of the form of judgement

Procedures of Tarrying

and the suspended mode of representation also lead the way to a new field of investigation in which certain analyses first become possible. Discourse in the twentieth century found support in sustained tarrying, which provides key methodological concepts for an understanding of how to investigate a discursive field and its presuppositions, cultural practices and their possibilities, and the knowledge's cohesion and formation. It might seem hazardous to orient the work of the so-called humanities towards a discipline of tarrying but therein lie both new starting points and technical tools. I will not conceal my sympathy for a methodologically trained tarrying but want to use this weakness for programmatic purposes.

Insofar as tarrying uncovers the problems and questions that correspond to existing situations and dilemmas, one programmatic procedure it implies is the interruption of the historical process and the resistance against mere continuation, thereby demonstrating that our mode of being and its conditions are contingent. Tarrying demands a critical ontology of our selves, of our beings, our discourses and thoughts. It distends and enlarges the present, thereby giving it a new shape that no longer appears inevitable and fixed. In this way, the limitations that circumscribe the event and determine the foundations of the knowing, judging and acting subject can be experienced as such. This will make more than obvious the fact that our present knowledge is as instable as its provenance is obscure, and that there is no guarantee that categories, disciplines and sciences will retain their present constitutions.

As apparent constants and verities are thereby pushed toward the edge of their becoming, their questionability can open up a historical project that insists on the inconclusiveness of history. In this historical view, the apparent division of discourses, for example into literature, science and other types of knowledge, is by no means uniform, recognizable and coherent; it requires a certain agnosticism. Just as tarrying destroys every eschatological substrate, so too it exempts history from its necessary course. The cartography of history reveals itself as a flow chart of branching paths; and the shape of disciplines, the hegemony of objects of knowledge, the design of systems of statements no longer appear as sustainable facts but as circumstances that have coalesced after massive alterations with alternative possibilities and options. This historical sense produces a doctrine of faculties and explores in historical discourses those forces, powers and movements that have produced their form and their limits. History and historical analysis refer to the changes of which a society is capable. Knowledge emerged from *polemos* and from fluctuating structures.

Methodical tarrying, therefore, contains a significant theoretical implication for the analysis of culture: a distinction between 'robust' and 'idiosyncratic' theories. While a robust theory always already knows its objects (like 'literature,' 'knowledge,' 'science,' 'reason') and, therefore, does not really need a theory, an idiosyncratic procedure presupposes the inexplicability of its objects and requires along with its analytical work a theoretical endeavour that concerns the adaptability

Idiosyncratic Theories

of its descriptions. An idiosyncratic method reduces and reflects on its normative presuppositions, and it minimizes the subsumptive force of its concepts. It does not pursue an assumed unity of its object but those distributions and migrations of knowledge that contribute to the constitution of objectivity, that make up the inner multiplicity of an object. Every object of knowledge is a palimpsest. An idiosyncratic theory, therefore, aims at a pagan knowledge, if 'pagan,' derived from the Latin *pagus*, refers to a local, limited and in no way globalizable field of knowledge. In that field, knowledge—contrary to a long Aristotelian tradition—is no longer knowledge of the universal. Rather, it requires an equally 'regional' and 'pluralistic' epistemology that allows for competing universalities with differing limits and applications.[7]

This also forms its relationship to history as critique. In contradistinction to a critical 'court' that specializes in the distinction between correct understanding and incorrect imagination,[8] it returns to the historicity of such forms of judgement and questions the positive limitations that enable events of universalization. No actual knowledge remains familiar when it is confronted with its provenance and its past. This requires the choice of a level of description that does not simply reproduce the teleologies and criteria of its objects; and it requires a mode of critique that interrupts its own tendency to generalize. It results from a historiographic enterprise that acquires its space for reflection not by questioning knowledge with respect to its essence, its nature, its foundation or its legitimacy, but with respect to its actuality: What must be the form of a knowledge of a history that produces the distinction between true and false upon which such knowledge relies?

The theme of tarrying, then, leads from an elementary figure of action to a doctrine of methods; it is buoyed by the conviction that a thorough analysis must search for the locus and the effectiveness of singular, contingent data in phenomena that impose themselves as necessary and binding. The pragmatism of this procedure, the pragmatism of a historical scent, holds fast to a doctrine of thresholds that acts as a permanent critique of our historical becoming. It may recommend itself as methodical tarrying and as a variant of the sense for historical possibilities—perhaps as part of a universal history of contingency. In contrast to philosophical imperturbability or *Gelassenheit* which willingly abdicates from willing, remains between Yes and No, and searches for a lasting moratorium in order 'to let everything merge in its own resting,'[9] methodical tarrying refuses to ignore the uncomfortable premonition that it has not become easier to believe, here and now, in this life and this world.

Notes

1   Kafka, *The Castle*, p. 53.

2   Kafka, *Blue Octavo Notebooks*, p. 87.

3   Dante, *Divine Comedy: Purgatory* (Canto 18). On the modern programmatics of *acaedia*, see Thomas Pynchon, 'Sloth' in Thomas Pynchon (ed.), *Deadly Sins* (New York: William Morrow & Co, 1993), pp. 10–23.

4   Kafka, *Blue Octavo Notebooks*, p. 55.

5 Essential reading on this subject is Samuel Weber, *Targets of Opportunity: On the Militarization of Thinking* (New York: Fordham University Press, 2005), especially pp. 1–21.

6 Hans Blumenberg, 'Die Heteronomie von "Freund" und "Feind"' ('The Hereteronomy of "Friend" and "Enemy"') in *Die Vollzähligkeit der Sterne* (Frankfurt: Suhrkamp, 1997), pp. 345–8.

7 Michel Serres, *Hermes II. Interferenz* (Berlin: Merve, 1992), pp. 10–11.

8 Plato, *Theaetetus*, 201c.

9 Martin Heidegger, *Discourse on Thinking* (John M. Anderson and E. Hans Freund trans) (New York: Harper and Row, 1966), pp. 58–9, 66–7, 74–5.